assed for change."

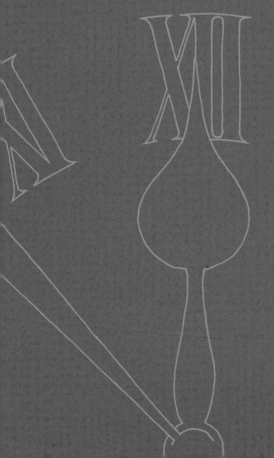

crisis of
confidence

crisis of
confidence

*utilities, public relations,
and credibility*

Frank C. Sullivan

 PHOENIX PUBLISHING
Canaan, New Hampshire

Sullivan, Frank C.   1900-
    Crisis of confidence.

    Bibliography: p. 123
    Includes indes.
        1.   Public utilities—United States. 2. Public
relations—United States. I. Title.
HD2766.S85   659.2′9′36360973   76-53983
ISBN 0-914016-36-9

Printed in the United States of America
by Courier Printing Company.
Binding by New Hampshire Bindery
Design by A. L. Morris

for Ruth

Acknowledgments and Permissions

Views expressed on pubic ownership and certain regulatory matters have appeared, in a different form, in articles in the PUBLIC UTILITIES FORTNIGHTLY.

The following publishers generously granted permission to quote from the works indicated:

Houghton Mifflin Company: John Kenneth Galbraith, THE NEW INDUS-TRIAL STATE and THE LIBERAL HOUR. Reprinted by permission of Houghton Mifflin Company.

LOS ANGELES TIMES: Martin Rossman, "Public Relations Executives Called Too Proud to Do Job," published May 2, 1972. Copyright, 1972, Los Angeles Times. Reprinted by permission.

LOS ANGELES TIMES: Harry Trimborn, "Wilson's Socialist Program Outlined by Queen," published October 30, 1974. Copyright, 1974, Los Angeles Times. Reprinted by permission.

Macmillan Publishing Co., Inc.: Michael Harrington, THE ACCIDENTAL CENTURY (Copyright© Michael Harrington 1965).

Simon & Schuster, Inc.: Will and Ariel Durant, LESSONS OF HISTORY, Copyright© 1968 by Will and Ariel Durant, published by Simon and Schuster.
TIME: Excerpts from "The Future of Free Enterprise," TIME Essay, February 14, 1972; Reprinted by permission from TIME, The Weekly Newsmagazine; Copyright Time Inc. 1972.

The publishers are deeply indebted to American Gas Association, New England Telephone, Southern California Gas Company, and Underwood, Jordan Associates for their help and cooperation in providing the photographs incorporated in the jacket design and used within this book. They are listed below as they appear on the dust jacket from left to right, with interleaf pages on which some appear also indicated.

Connecticut Yankee Atomic Power Company Reactor
    (Edison Electric Institute/Underwood, Jordan)
Hygas Purification System Tower
    (Institute of Gas Technology) Interleaf page 8
Traffic Service Position System
    (New England Telephone)
American Electric Power Systems Transmission Line
    (Edison Electric Institute/Underwood, Jordan)
Battery of Coin Operated Telephones
    (New England Telephone)
Aliso Canyon Underground Storage Field
    (Southern California Gas Company) Interleaf page 92
Alamitos Steam-Electric Station
    (Southern California Edison Company/Underwood, Jordan) Interleaf page 38
Segment of 4A Toll Switching Machine
    (New England Telephone) Interleaf page 64
Consumers' Gas Company Offshore Drilling Rig
    (American Gas Association)

CONTENTS

Foreword

SCRATCH ANY business executive these days and you wound a harried man. Beset in many quarters, he has a feeling of being adrift in perilous waters without rudder or compass, and he yearns for the "good old days," dreaming nostalgically of the halcyon time before the coming of the second Roosevelt.

He understands his business . . .how to create, sell and manage . . .for he may rightfully claim the distinction of being the canniest entrepreneur in the entire world. He understands almost everything in the milieu in which he functions so admirably, but some things he cannot understand. For example, people in the mass and what motivates their current views of the social order, particularly their increasingly active and vocal lack of confidence in business and those who direct its destinies. For another, the restrictive actions of government, an apparent capricious and lunatic infringement of a bumbling bureaucracy on the rights of the private sector. Yet another, the persistent and sometimes virulent antagonism of the communication media, themselves a part of the very economic system they decry so often.

As he ponders these signs of the times he knows that something is wrong in a turbulent America, caught in a vortex of change affecting customs and ideas. He can console himself with the fact that Americans are far from *united* for change for even the last

Presidential election revealed that those who still cling to the old values and the status quo are legion. But even the most conservative of those who inhabit the executive suites of the land are aware of a massive divergency of thought regarding our present and future direction, and must acknowledge an unpromising trend of public opinion for those who wear gray flannel suits.

Everyone knows that nothing is static, and change is as inevitable as man's death. The concern is, what sort of change impends . . .and how swiftly? More to the point, what can be done to shape its form and substance and give it reasonable direction? At the heart of this question lies a need for understanding the nature of the problem, the subtleties of the social interdependencies which have created it, and recognition of the need for new thought and responsive action.

This book deals principally with the role of the public utility in the business sector, and specifically with its patterns of communications in this turbulent era of changing public opinion. No better protagonist for such examination could be found, for no other unit of the free enterprise system is more intimately in touch with its publics or more directly subject to government control. As a corollary, if most business units are compelled these days to frequently wear the hair shirt of public criticism or prolonged public disfavor, the utility is apt to itch more readily, more often, and for longer periods.

The reasons for this are enumerated in the text that follows. But the broader point is that the business establishment itself confronts a crisis of confidence which may herald profound changes in our thinking and our lives, for better or worse. It requires no feat of logic to apply to the whole the lessons to be learned from one of its parts.

crisis of
confidence

Prologue

A Rationale for Action

THE PRACTICE of public relations has come a long way in the past fifty years from hit or miss publicity to depth interviews, where one's purchase of a household appliance may be predicated on his sexual fantasies.

It was fifty years ago that I first heard the words when, a youthful reporter on a California newspaper, I was sent by the City Editor to cover the arrival of the great Ivy Lee in our town.

The very mention of his name, I now recall, must have evoked in me the same sort of hero worship that stirred young Browning: "Ah, did you once see Shelley plain. . .?"

Ivy Lee was no Shelley, I no Browning, but the analogy may be apt: to me, he dwelt upon the mountaintop.

The great man—a not immodest designation for this celebrity fresh from his Rockefeller triumphs—arrived in a private Pullman, which was switched to a siding, after which he regally disembarked with his wife and several children, swathed to the ears in a long overcoat against the chill of a Sacramento spring morning, *wearing a homburg and carrying a cane elegantly hooked over an arm.*

This visitation was prompted by his interest in art: he had come to inspect the famed Crocker Art Gallery. Although quite overwhelmed by the homburg *and* cane, as well as by the odor of affluence pervading the person of the visitor as certainly as incense permeates a joss house, I managed to mumble a few simple questions designed to develop a lead for my story.

Strangely, considering a man with his towering reputation for verbal felicity and sharp—not to say, devious—intellect, he was monosyllabic with his replies. As a matter of fact, he conveyed the undeniable impression that my efforts to interrogate him were impeding his progress toward consummating the business which had enticed him from the seclusion of his private car.

I did contrive to have my cameraman snap a group picture of him and his family. This was duly published, together with an account of his fleeting stopover, which it was necessary to embellish, in the absence of memorable quotes, with a few imaginative comments of my own.

Nonetheless, for the record, it was that day I had heard the siren words "public relations" and had seen in the flesh its earliest, shrewdest, and most legendary practitioner.

As a footnote, some twenty-five years later I met and became the friend of Ivy Lee, Jr., presently an able San Francisco public relations executive—the little boy who had stood bashfully at the extreme edge of the family group when the picture was taken.

The seed planted that raw spring day sprouted ten years later when I abandoned a secure but dead-end job on the re-write staff of another California newspaper, and embarked upon the stormy seas of public relations. That was in 1934, a starvation time for many, and I lacked two of the three necessities listed cynically by Irwin Ross in his book, *The Image Merchants*—namely, "a client, a typewriter, and a mimeograph machine."[1] The typewriter I had; the other two came later.

My office, a cheerless, rugless room in a downtown office building, had on its door—"Publicity, Campaigns, Advertising." (Later experience confirmed an early instinct that a fancy office is not required by the public relations free-lancer, in contrast to the requirements of an advertising agency, a doctor, a lawyer, or even a chiropractor. Reason: clients *rarely* visit the PR worker—he visits *them*.)

In the early Depression years it was "publicity" and the jousting ground for this was in the news columns of the daily and weekly press. We lived and died on the smiles or frowns of the various editors—city, managing, financial, sports, and so on. Television was an amusing fantasy, confined to the Buck Rogers realm of the funny papers, for who in his right mind could imagine transmitting pictures through the air? Although radio was a well-respected entertainment medium, used for press releases upon occasion and as an afterthought, it was mainly print media that beguiled our thinking, leading us to concoct stories for our clients that were designed to masquerade as "news" and accepted as such by the editors.

News stories were then regarded with a less critical eye for veracity than is the case nowadays. I clearly remember my first few days on the rewrite battery of a certain metropolitan newspaper when, after the final edition had been locked up and it was time to work on "overnight" for the next day's early street edition, the city editor tossed on my desk several eight by ten glossies of beautiful girls, furnished by a wire service, and in various stages of undress. "Give us something to carry them," he said. Mystified, I sought enlightenment from the grizzled veteran at an adjoining desk. "Oh," he shrugged, "just make up something."

He was already engaged in "making up something," and so I followed, allowing my imagination full rein, with stories of Palm Beach beauties escaping from marital misadventures in northern climes, of lovely ladies robbed of jewels by "cat" burglars, and similar lurid nonsense which, along with other colorful tales created by my colleagues, duly appeared in the following day's first run. Such published canards accompanied the wire service "art." As hard news developed during the later hours after the first edition, our fictional absurdities were killed by the news editor; but the practice of writing and using these fillers extended over into the publicity field and provided a certain latitude of expression for the press agent.

Clem Whitaker, Sr. had come to San Francisco about this time from Sacramento, where he had been engaged in news reporting for a San Francisco afternoon newspaper, and in handling political campaigns on a part-time basis. It was in San Francisco that he sharpened his techniques for managing such campaigns, and where he developed patterns and procedures still aped with almost undeviating devotion by campaign directors today. It was my fortune to work for him in his San Francisco office for a brief period and, when I opened my own office in Oakland, to direct his political operations in the counties east of San Francisco Bay.

Not until a dozen years later had we in the western United States graduated upward, as it were, to the use of the term "public relations" to describe our fledgling efforts to achieve somewhat intangible ends. In this respect, our tardiness placed us about 127 years behind Thomas Jefferson who used—possibly coined—the phrase in his seventh Congressional address in October, 1807, and a few decades behind Theodore Vail, Ivy Lee, and others of the early gentry.

Similarly, those were the days before opinion polls, depth interviewing, enunciation of objectives, selection of publics, and the doubting acceptance of the bizarre pronouncement of Dr. Dichter that a man buys an automobile, selects a household appliance, or a set of tires, and wears a certain suit of clothes, all because of the subconscious yearnings of his libido.

Nor had we yet supported the still somewhat novel concept that the practice of public relations entitles the person so equipped to sit in corporate board rooms or at presidential right hands and speak, although not necessarily be spoken to.

The progress of the art, or occupation or—if you will momentarily accept it—"profession," has been long and rocky, frequently marked by road blocks and detours.

There are substantial and perhaps readily understandable reasons for this. One, of course, is the aura of intangibility that still hovers over certain public relations enterprises, at times, as contrasted to the down-to-earth techniques of paid sales advertising where you either ring the cash register, or you do not.

Yet the fact is incontrovertible that when the corporate roof caves in, as it frequently does these days, what with vocal ecological and consumer groups, dissident stockholders, demagogic government and crippling legislation, various and sundry attacks against the "Establishment" by minorities and others quite properly demanding larger slices of the income pie—when the corporate going is very, very rough—an expert, intelligent, soundly grounded public relations advisor is worth his weight in rubies.

There are such literate fellows, but let it also be plainly stated that perhaps in no other gainful occupation, save such as astrology, chiropractic, or Elmer Gantry evangelism, have so many charlatans managed to find a toehold. In no other field, except possibly that of the surgeon, is there such a marked difference in the results achievable through an expert or a clumsy performance.

The Public Relations Society of America, Inc., through its accreditation program, conceived and nurtured through its infancy by that able practitioner, G. Edward Pendray, has striven mightily to prescribe and maintain standards tending to support the premise that there is an ascertainable difference between the competent and the fraudulent in public relations.

There is, of course. This gulf yawns as widely as the Grand Canyon; but whether the Society's effort has succeeded in either properly measuring or spanning this chasm remains the subject of considerable debate among the discerning. Regrettably for those truly skilled, not all members of top management are sufficiently knowledgable to distinguish the difference between the true and the meretricious.

Consequently, the ranks of public relations, as any qualified practitioner knows full well, are sprinkled with what appears more than a fair share of incompetents and sometimes originally from such disparate and honorable callings as law, business administration, accounting, finance, and personnel.

The former, the out-and-out incompetents, have learned that a personable appearance and a glib tongue with a gift for platitudinous jargon may frequently compensate for fundamental inadequacies as indeed they often do. The latter, those fugitives from another field, see no particular reason why they should not function in this presumably glamorous and relatively new occupation, where, after all, the ability to shake hands and slap backs, plus the knack of conversing wittily at cocktail parties and holding one's liquor, may be accepted as a cachet of public relations erudition.

This advancement of the incompetent, or the mountebank trespasser, due largely to myopic management, has long plagued more than a few American utilities. Perhaps in no other leading area of business has management so often been seduced by engineers and attorneys hankering for public relations posts or for supervision of public relations staffs, as in the utility industry.

One is hard pressed to explain such managerial enchantment except upon the admittedly nebulous premise that these managements tend to *understand* law, engineering, economics, accounting, the *established* professions, through everyday familiarity. The professional disciplines invoked seek and provide pat solutions to pat problems in a realistic world, in striking contrast to the often iffy proposals of public relations. The result is that today many a hardnosed, no-nonsense, prove-it-to-me utility executive regards the public relations function as a management sport, smacking slightly of witchcraft, and imbued with gossamer-like fantasies woven by starry-eyed dreamers. Others, witnessing results, support and defend PR.

The reference here, of course, is to public relations in its rarefied form—its true form, its distilled essence.

Everyone, even those utility executives not attuned to the nuances of the public relations world, understands that you require "someone who writes" to perform such homely chores as editing a house organ, or a management news bulletin, or writing and placing a news release, or arranging radio and/or television interviews, or devising the graphic layout for a brochure, or whatever. The list of nuts and bolts is an endless one, and it is noteworthy that it is not in this area that interlopers or top management itself aspire to an expertise they do not possess.

No, the tasks mentioned are journeymen tasks, ones, it is true, on which many workers spend frustrating lives, both within corporations and the agencies which service them. One hastens to add that for the miseries of these worthies we should scarcely heave a passing sigh, let alone shed a commiserative tear, for the jobs mentioned are honorable and necessary, and someone must perform them. Philosophically, those determined to ascend the public relations ladder which ultimately may lead to the mountaintop of counseling must first learn to climb.

Besides, to repeat, those are not the accomplishments the untrained, the posturer, the invader from another field, and the highly placed executive himself, yearn to undertake or to supervise. They are not the ones over whom gallons of corporate blood are spilled on lush carpets in executive suite vendettas which are as vicious in their way as the attacks of frenzied barracuda.

The tasks which count, really count, are the more complex and hence more difficult of resolution. They are those life and death matters where the corporate future is laid on the line in the manner of the Las Vegas crapshooter staking his all on the fateful seven; or where there exists thrust and counter-thrust of maneuvcrable events in the corporate jungle—where the considered advice, once given, can not be recalled or changed—where such advice may and probably will jeopardize one's job by subjecting the daring advisor to instant challenge by his executive peers should the ploy prove abortive.

There is a question as to whether this *kind* of public relations can be taught. Its practice seems to rest largely upon instinct grounded in experience. However, there are many excellent works in the public relations bibliography which may be used as textbooks for the elementary tasks, and a number of higher institutions of learning now turn out graduates who understand the basics.

The assumption made here is that the reader is beyond the elementary and involved with public utilities and their common public relations problems. No pretense will be made that recourse to these pages will enable the reader to tap freely a source of Delphic wisdom—for nobody commands such wisdom. On the other hand, one may come to a comprehension of the commonality of utilities' problems in their relationships to their publics, and learn something of how they have been met, are being met, and the requirements for meeting them in the future.

A word by way of personal bias: it is my long held conviction that the best basic experience for those in public relations at any level is to have worked for a newspaper at one time in his career. The techniques of news gathering, assembling, and writing; the distillation of news material to its essentials, and an understanding of public reaction to events, develop in the newsman an uncanny instinct which becomes a priceless asset in the kit bag of the public relations worker.

It is this instinct upon which the PR man must often call when offering a value judgment in a critical moment. But it must be acknowledged that far more than instinct is needed in today's world of complex forces governing the successful communication of ideas.

Public Relations
and
the Utility

1

In the Beginning

LET NO ONE assume that the introduction of the public relations function into the corporate structure of public utilities has been without its danger and wounds for practitioners.

As with any novel concept, particularly one proclaiming the idea that community esteem may be created by the utilization of artful communications techniques linked to acts, there have been detractors. Any disparagements have been compounded by the fact that utilities' managements have not always been noted for their innovative characteristics. If investigative psychologists are to be believed, quite the contrary may be the case.

Not too long ago the president of a major utility, evidently aspiring to a mantle of progressive leadership, decided to employ an industrial psychologist to probe the personalities of his immediate staff, which consisted mainly of vice-presidents with a few middle management executives added for seasoning. The subjects, most of them reluctant but timidly submissive, were interviewed in due course. They were required to answer long and involved questionnaires, containing built-in lie detection traps, with such queries as: "Did you love your mother?" "When in grammar school, did you ever play hooky?" "Did you ever steal—such as apples from a neighbor's orchard?" "How do you like to work—alone or with a group?"

Many of those interrogated failed to fathom the relevancy of this catechism to their managerial duties, but they judged that failure to participate would open them to the suspicion of something, they knew not what.

Each tested individual was privately furnished an interpretive report by the examiner, who was at pains to pledge that its secrecy was as inviolate as that of the confessional. Later, when certain expected promotions failed to materialize, cynics wondered about these protestations, but the group finding was significant.

"Viewed as a whole," reported the psychologist, "these people are unimaginative and dignified—not to say stuffy. They resemble bankers, more than any other management group I have surveyed."

Introducing esoteric public relations personnel and their offbeat endeavors into such utilities cadres was bound to raise questions and eyebrows, but there was no choice. After World War II, it became increasingly clear to industry leaders that their story must be effectively told—not only singly through each individual corporation, but simultaneously and collectively through national trade associations, formed mainly by the gas and electric utilities, or by "combination" companies which distributed both forms of energy. History records that the electric companies led the vanguard of the national effort to develop and conduct sophisticated public relations programs, with others not too far behind.

In the initial local and national efforts, the company sales functions were often established in positions of authority, and therefore leadership, much to the discomfiture and chagrin of public relations professionals who had, as it were, battled their way to the magic kingdom of acceptance only to find the donjon locked against them. In the early days it was not uncommon for vice-presidents of sales to represent their companies at conferences called to formulate national programs, sometimes with communications executives present but serving in inferior committee positions. This arrangement was a natural outgrowth of the budding status of the public relations function in the single companies where, at first, it was considered by senior management to be subordinate to, and an appendage of, the sales program. Personnel of sales seized this functional windfall with comprehensible satisfaction. With the passage of time and the multiplication of problems occasioned by the need for compensatory rates, by the rise of articulate consumerism, and by public suspicion of the objectivity of regulation, there was a change in official attitude. Domination by sales departments vanished and in the utilities industry creation and retention of goodwill came of age.

Even so, nascent doubts of the integrity of the new profession persisted within many companies. These were nursed not only by those associating it with press agent puffery but by some journalists as well, who exhibited resentment possibly triggered by jealousy of this upstart cousin in communications offering fatter paychecks.

As an example of the first category, consider John Kenneth Galbraith's 1958 polemic on Henry Ford, whose credentials as an authentic genius of American industry he considered fraudulent.

Charging in *The Liberal Hour* that Ford was the "product of a pioneer public relations ploy," Galbraith continues:

Since Ford's time public relations has become our youngest profession. No great executive's personality or ideas are now released to the public without extensive retouching. We have made our accommodation to this—although it is not one that is entirely advantageous to the businessman. Not knowing what to believe we have resolved where the executive is concerned to believe nothing. . .It is distressing to discover that the Ford myth is the first of the industrial fairy tales—not in total, of course, but in considerable part.[2]

Mr. Galbraith paints—one hesitates to observe "as usual"— with too broad a brush. Besides, since Ford's day, as our recent history will bear witness, print and electronic media have become viciously adept at pillorying the meretricious. Straw men are exposed, windbags deflated, liars castigated, all in the pitiless spotlight of public scrutiny. This is not the age of the hero but the anti-hero.

Aside from the inquisitorial temper of the times, assuring protection against the planned puffery of an individual as well as the cynical debunking of issues, there is the bulwark provided by the considerations of professionalism. The best public relations workers now publicly espouse and privately practice the principle that trust and goodwill can not be won and retained save on a truthful basis. To this assertion there must be a caveat: silence, sometimes necessary to invoke as a refuge, does not *necessarily* equate with chicanery.

Some of the caustic criticism by Galbraith and others may have become self-perpetuating myths through repetition, yet it can not be denied that newspapermen are at times more sour than Galbraith, evidenced by a survey quoted in the August, 1975, issue of the *Public Relations Journal*, national organ of the Public Relations Society of America, Inc.

Although 89 percent of public relations practitioners queried agreed that public relations and the press are "partners in the dissemination of information," only 59 percent of newsmen agreed and 39 percent disavowed the relationship. When it came to the question of whether practitioners help reporters obtain accurate, complete, and timely news, 91 percent of the practitioners attested to the truth of the statement, but 44 percent of the journalists churlishly disagreed. Other replies by newspapermen were similarly discouraging for the egos of practitioners; so discouraging, in fact, that one acquainted with the very substantial services rendered the press by PR people could suspect that newsmen's hostilities might be motivated by envy of their better paid brothers. Whatever the motive, most of those in public relations are aware they are viewed with supercilious eyes by many of their news writing associates, a fact which defies rational explanation since many—perhaps most—of the better public relations specialists are hatched in newspaper editorial rooms.

The fairly widespread acceptance of Galbraith's thinking which may have become part of contemporary wisdom, coupled with the adverse views of influential communicators and the early growth of public relations without academic benediction, make it easy to understand why there was doubt and even distrust among starchy utilities executives when this new square was marked on management organization charts.

In fine, utilities regarded public relations with nervous skepticism in the beginning. Today, its tasks are the most crucial facing the companies—not even excluding those of finance and law.

2

Public Relations: What?

L EADERS and management executives of the public utilities industry have often paraphrased Pontius Pilate's question: "What is truth?" by amending it to "What is public relations?"

Some of them have frequently followed this query with another — a skeptical, "Why?"

Only two decades ago there were many such leaders and executives. Although today there are relatively few, in management offices the nagging suspicion persists that this function of public relations is, as the saying goes, pretty far out in several respects.

For many years and until recently, one large "combination" company — perhaps the largest utility in the United States — did not have a public relations department as such, although several employees were engaged daily in performing public relations functions. The revulsion to the usage of the term public relations was so overpowering in the mind of this utility's board chairman that he forbade the words to be lettered upon the department's door. As a result, the public relations people, who were engaged in community relations, governmental affairs, news writing, radio, television, and magazine work, were required to conduct their activities under the banner of "publicity and advertising," which the chairman deemed a nomenclature sufficiently specific to connote usefulness.

A few years ago the chairman's tenure was terminated by death. Whether his departure changed the designation on the department's door the present record does not disclose, but because of what might be charitably characterized as terminological ineptitude, the public relations activities of that particular utility always seemed to be somehow inhibited.

There are many definitions of public relations, most of them satisfactory, although candor compels the acknowledgment that the words are sometimes used to conceal, instead of clarify, a function in a very complex business society.

The lobbyist whose job is to contact any public official from the city poundmaster to a presidential assistant on behalf of a favor for his client directly or indirectly carries the words "public relations" on his business card. So does the professional speaker for a cause or group; the press agent for a movie star or for the zoo's trained dolphins; the fund raiser for the church, the university, or the politician. The list of those identified with public relations is endless and fascinating. The late Arthur Samish, California's most noted and notorious lobbyist, was engaged in "public relations," he said upon occasion, but an even more fanciful example might be cited. This was the case of a buxom lady who became an associate member of the San Francisco Chapter of the Public Relations Society of America. One evening at a chapter session she produced her professional card: "Mrs. Blank — Mimeograph Supplies — Carbon Paper — All Office Needs."

The standards of qualification are changing, particularly in the professional society which is aware of the dangers to status involved in admitting the unqualified. Developing standards and adhering to definitions every year further clarify what public relations is and is not.

Basically, the task comes down to establishing and retaining public goodwill for your client, whether a corporation or an individual. Some have called this "creation of a good image" for the client in the collective mind of the public. This is undertaken by utilizing the arts and procedures of modern communication techniques through media. The method may range anywhere from a newspaper story or advertisement, or a paid or free television appearance, to winking lights on the underbelly of the Goodyear blimp. Going a step further, it also means advising your client on what positive moves he may make — or not make — in the public interest which might serve as fodder for the communications mill. As an example, President Nixon's visits to the Mid-East and to Moscow during the height of the Watergate controversy might be regarded as public relations moves of the highest order, attracting as they did the spotlight of favorable publicity.

In the technical sense, the purest and most difficult practice of public relations creates a client's strategy. The generous disbursement of dimes to children by the original Rockefeller at the suggestion of Ivy Lee to counter the magnate's reputed penchant for penuriousness is a classic case in point. Such creation of public statement or movement demands a battle commander's sense of timing, a sociologist's sensitivity to shifting tides of public opinion, and an acute awareness of political forces as well as the psychology of politicians as men first and public figures second. Along with these, the better practitioner has become either a conscious or unconscious student of the behavioral sciences; "unconscious" because some —even many — through experience wedded to instinct, *know* what public reaction to a statement or an event will be ahead of time. This faculty often borders on the miraculous. It is one that utility executives trained in other fields find particularly surprising.

There are as many formal definitions of public relations as there are practitioners of the art, for experts tend sometimes to disagree like those early travelers who first described the elephant. One saw its ears, another its trunk, another its tail, suggesting that everything is in the point of view.

Certain basic procedures are common to almost all *true* public relations approaches, such as the opinion sampling (which ever becomes more accurate), statement of objectives, analysis of problems, development of budget, departmental organization, checkup of results, etc. Beyond these formalities, however, the solution to a specific, complex problem often lies in improvisation resting on the experience and native skill of the public relations executive. As an analogy, on a far higher level of course, Raphael, Titian, Renoir, and Rembrandt all painted beautiful pictures and all used the common tools of brushes, oils, and canvas, yet each brought to his work something very personal; a unique creative power not subject to analysis. The better public relations executive brings to a problem just such a personal creative approach, grounded in experience. For this reason the public relations executive, even if

lacking specialized knowledge or academic backg
never shrink from becoming an innovator if the bre
trail seems necessary.

A definition of public relations perhaps better th
cause it synthesizes several from various sources—
by Denny Griswold, the editor of *Public Relations*
standard volume, *Your Public Relations.*

> *Public relations is the management function which ev*
> *lic attitudes, identifies the policies and procedures of (*
> *or an organization with the public interest, and execu*
> *of action to earn public understanding and acceptar*

This is full of operative words: *managen*
evaluates, identifies, public interest, executes, acceptance.

Thus, the definition denotes the ideal of what public relations
is or ought to be. Sometimes because of one stumbling block or
another we can not always conform to the ideal. Frequently, the
function does not rate very high on the utility management chart. In
too many instances it is regarded as an appendage of the sales and
marketing function. Upon occasion, a utility may also have a slight
difficulty in identifying its necessary policy or action with the
immediate public interest, as contrasted to the company interest.
On the whole, however, the definition represents a solid platform
upon which to build a public relations program.

The so-called "tools" of public relations are something else.

Recently a mailing from New York City offered a *Professional's
Guide to Public Relations Services,*[3] containing, so the blurb an-
nounced, "614 public relations services every PR man *must* use."
(Emphasis supplied.) Included in this work were: 83 clipping
bureaus, 41 literary services, 24 mailing services, 40 media direc-
tories, 11 VIP services, 10 packaged publicity services, 27 photo and
fine art services, 17 messenger services, 18 photography services,
17 motion picture distributors, 20 radio and TV services, 25 prize
contests, promotions, and giveaways, and 17 mat services.

With all of these at one's beck and call, how could one fail to
communicate? The key to effective communication, of course, is to
utilize the most effective means available, considering timeliness
and budget, the latter a most important element since there comes a
point where cost may render the effort counterproductive.

No company, of course, requires *all* of the 614 services offered in the "professional's guide."

A general listing of media available to the utility for internal communication would include: employee newspapers and magazines; management publications for supervisors; letters, notices or memoranda to various levels of company executives; bulletin board notices; motion pictures and slide presentations for training or policy indoctrination; talks by managers; jobholder meetings; and bulletins to retired employees.

For its external publics: newspaper releases which are uncontrollable after issue since they are subject to editorial alteration or distortion; television and radio news publicity, having the same deficiency; public relations advertising, controllable but with the possible taint of being self-serving; pamphlets, bill stuffers, annual reports and other print media of varied assortment such as billboards and car cards. Each is suitable for a specific purpose: one medium for heavy or flash impact for example, another to inform each customer of a specific, another as supplementary to a general campaign, and so on.

The public relations firm of Bergen & Lee in Los Angeles, evidently finding difficulties in explaining to prospective clients what public relations is — and is not — recently produced and distributed a pretentious pamphlet titled: "What in the (expletive deleted) is this public relations jazz?" and later, on the title page: "An answer (with no expletives deleted) from Bergen & Lee, Inc."

Frankly, say the authors, *there are all kinds of P.R. – Press relations. Community relations. Investor relations. Product publicity. Image building. Consumer relations. Special events. Etcetera. But all kinds of effective P.R. have one thing in common: They sell. An image. A product. A service. An idea. Good public relations is not a cover-up. If anything, it's an open-up. Because one cannot change attitudes with silence; only with effort.*

The pamphlet continues with the exhortation: "Find out where your firm has been and where it is today. With your employees. Your community. Your customers. Your potential customers. Your stockholders. Your peers. The press."

And finally the promise: "A full-service P.R. firm can do that for you."

How?

Well, says Bergen & Lee, Inc.,

Maybe you need those press releases. And maybe you don't. Maybe you need that special event. And maybe you don't. Maybe you need to look over your volunteer activities and make some changes. And maybe you don't. In any event, the right thing to do is . . . the thing you need *to do* (Emphasis in original.)

Thus, the necessity to explain the function and the hope that a prospective client will come to understand it.

3

Public Relations—Why?

ALL UTILITY management executives should readily understand the requirement for strong and effective public relations programs. Many do not and even among those whose companies prosecute such programs there are some who reluctantly and grudgingly support funds for the task. They simply can not agree on the practical need for the function. But to other more perceptive executives there is something appalling in this attitude, for they are fully, perhaps painfully, aware of the climate in which the utility must perform its public service.

Speaking of the views of business generally, Scott M. Cutlip, author of textbooks on public relations and visiting professor at the Henry W. Grady School of Journalism of the University of Georgia, contends that the "public relations function remains misunderstood, undervalued, and under-utilized." At the same time, he lays at the door of public relations itself much of the responsibility for this, saying that too often he has observed the failure of public relations practitioners to measure up to the role defined for them by the urgent needs of today's world.

Aside from the "urgent needs" of today's world and today's corporations, the utility has certain special needs which cry out for public understanding, and it is these special needs which suggest utilities should be in the vanguard of public relations effort.

For one thing, the utility is especially vulnerable to public takeover because of its monopolistic nature. For another, it is usually under some type of public regulation and hence must rely upon public agencies for compensatory rates. These agencies, more often than not, and despite the frequent claims of antagonistic crusaders, have their official ears finely attuned to the people's objections to rate increases. While such objections may sometimes be rooted in the selfish resistance of the individual utility customer to pay more for anything he might conceivably obtain for less, they usually result from ignorance of the utility's financial need, which must be *persuasively* presented in the court of public opinion.

It is axiomatic in both utility and regulatory circles that public pressures have a tendency to induce regulatory agencies to establish rates in the *lower*, not the higher, zones of reasonableness. There are occasions on which agency members, either elected or appointed, may wish to battle against this tide. If they do, their impulses toward generosity are often balked by their own staff members, who almost always tip the balance of the regulatory scales against the interests of the utility and its shareholders. In sum, the application by the utility to obtain compensatory rates in the face of countervailing public support—or at least acquiescence—is only attainable through using public relations techniques. Members of agencies have welcomed a better public understanding of why higher rates are sought during inflation; but agency employees, usually protected from the vicissitudes of job competition by civil service, evince little interest in public attitudes, although, in most cases, coming down on the side of the consumer.

One of the historical public opinion problems confronted by some utilities, particularly those providing natural gas and water, is what might be characterized as an aberration in the public mind. One opinion survey after another has emphasized the finding that many Americans are convinced natural gas and water, sometimes even electricity, are resources of nature to which everyone is entitled access without cost—or at a minimal price. The recent rise of articulate consumerism has served to accentuate that view.

This particular public viewpoint continuously surfacing in depth interview studies carries a frustrating message for utility executives. For utility management has been fighting a losing

20   *Crisis of Confidence*

rearguard action for the past decade against rising costs of equipment, basic raw materials, wages, and the cost of borrowed money. All have been going up, while the actual supply of energy has been declining. Water, once the cheapest and most plentiful of all resources, is actually becoming scarce, so that those areas which have been blessed with ample supplies tend to hoard those supplies against the demand of less fortunate sections of the country. In the natural gas industry, the days of bargain sales have long since ended, no longer is natural gas a "flared" or throwaway fuel. On the contrary, gas utilities are conducting worldwide hunts for the fuel, and paying almost any price once it is found and available for transport to the United States. Symptomatic of the trend is the fact that gas company sales departments have begun to offer "marketing services" as a substitute for the former aggressive sales campaigns of only a few years ago. Electric companies have long since harnessed water power and thus exhausted once bountiful hydro-produced energy. Bedevilled by the plaints of ecologists, they too roam the world for steam plant fuels at outrageously high prices, and contend with sometimes unreasonable public officials for permits to construct nuclear reactors. Telephone companies suffer from always higher equipment costs caused by a burgeoning population and technological advances. Most city transportation systems have long since gone bankrupt or turned to government as a savior.

Faced with these rising costs, utilities are usually on a collision course with consumer groups, public bodies, and politically sensitive elected officials who include city councils, city attorneys, boards of supervisors, members of state legislatures, governors, state and federal commissions, many of whom seek political kudos or advancement by essaying the role of David to the utility company's Goliath.

Always, hovering over this contest, is the specter of public ownership, a final resort for the disaffected ready to cry: "Their rates are too high. Let's float a bond issue and take them over!"

Consider the constant cost inflation in all sectors: equipment, wages, supply! The continuous and repetitive need for higher rates from the consuming public! Articulate consumerism, to which the news media give increasing attention! Compliant government, sometimes demagogic government, at various levels—and the omnipresent threat of public ownership! Add to these what seems an ever widening distrust of business *and* government, and always the possibility of more inflation or a depression.

These are a few of the compelling reasons why utilities should support strong programs of public relations—intelligently conceived and honestly and truthfully promulgated.

4

Organization

WITH RARE exceptions, the creation and development of public utilities' public relations departments are based on practical requirements.

The print media—is it necessary to answer their questions or to issue publicity releases? If the answer is "Yes," you must employ a publicist.

Community relations—clubs, chambers of commerce, schools—all the myriad elements which comprise thought-leading groups of the American town or city demand careful and expert consideration, as well as programs to meet genuine community needs.

Electronic journalism—television and radio—have brought a new dimension and specialized techniques to news gathering and presentation, and so someone knowledgeable must handle this.

Internal communications, both at an employee and an executive level, must be dealt with.

Politics—the nomination and election of government officials at various levels who, at times, exercise almost life and death control of a corporation; the work of personal contact with political agencies to advance the company's viewpoint—is an area always of vital importance, and someone must be responsible.

To segment the operation on a more generalized basis, most utilities executives agree on what has been termed the "three Cs approach"—customer and community relations, communications.

From these broad groupings, departmental organizations take off into the stratosphere, depending mainly upon the size of the company and the creative imagination of the personnel manager or whoever is in charge of selecting titles. On occasion, the supervisor of public relations has the rank of vice-president of one kind or another—hopefully of public relations—although as already stated, he is more likely to be a director or manager. One recalls the case of a public relations manager who, carrying that title, headed his company's PR activities for twenty years until in what could hardly be characterized as a precipitous action, his company elected him vice-president.

From the key supervisory position whatever its title, there may stem three or four subordinate positions. In community relations it might be a director, manager, or supervisor and in public and employee information the same although personnel information is a touchy subject with personnel managers who may battle bitterly to seize or retain this function. Then there is public affairs, a catchall term to describe the employee in charge of influencing public bodies, from city council up to regulatory agencies and United States senators—maybe even the President of the United States. In the unlikely event any of these extremely high level contacts were imperative, the "public affairs" representative would probably simply pave the way for a major company executive to confer with the august personage.

In some companies public relations has been wholly translated into public affairs and, if this is the case, the entire department will probably be headed by a "vice-president of public affairs." In a few executive circles this designation is regarded as lending an aura of distinction and the same comment would hold true for the title of "vice-president of corporate affairs." Public affairs and corporate affairs are words connoting momentous responsibilities and they do fall pleasantly upon the ear, somewhat like the use of "mortician" for "undertaker."

Shareholder relations is sometimes placed within the purview of the chief PR executive, at other times with a financial vice-president, occasionally with an outside agency which specializes in this area, or it can be retained by the chief executive officer himself.

Then there is a host of other duties: plant tours, motion

picture production (which is usually farmed out to technical experts), exhibits and displays, speech writing, and pamphlet preparation.

In smaller companies, a very few people will have responsibility for the many tasks falling within the general field of public relations. In the larger companies, duties are cut into small pieces like a Roman coin, but all are integrated under a single supervisor responsible to senior management.

In companies of all sizes the chief executive officer will usually play a crucial role in the public relations task—as he should—for it is in his office suite that the ultimate responsibility must rest.

Many departments simply grew as demand for specific services was recognized by management. As an example, during the rising cost period of 1952, with the resultant squeeze on earnings and tardy rate relief by regulatory bodies, one major utility with no experience in public relations undertook a somewhat timorous program of public contact work. Soon the company added a company magazine, and shortly afterward employed a public relations director. With these initial departures from the norm, things began to happen. Today, this utility has eighty employees in its public relations department. It has a professional as vice-president of public relations. It has won a number of awards and is recognized nationally for the general excellence and sophistication of its efforts in the field of building goodwill.

Yet when this utility first put a hesitant toe into the public relations pond, it had no plans for venturing deeper. One step led to another. As need became apparent, personnel were recruited to meet that need. Other utilities have followed the same pattern, to a greater or lesser degree.

One result in the larger utilities is a departmental organization highly structured and frequently complex. As a somewhat typical example, in examining one major utility, we find that the department is headed by a vice-president, whose sole responsibility is the multi-faceted public relations program. This officer reports to the president, while responsible to him are: two executive assistants by title who are actually legislative advocates guarding the company interests at the state legislative level; a manager of community relations; a manager of public and employee information; and a public affairs supervisor.

Reporting to the manager of community relations are: a

supervisor of community programs, and subordinate to him are three senior community services representatives; three community relations coordinators, whose tasks lie in organizing plant and installation tours; a supervisor of school programs, who has three assistants; a contributions administrator, whose job is to review requests from the hosts of charities which assault the checkbooks of public utilities; and a lone urban affairs representative, assigned to work among minority groups and build an "image" for the utility as a fair employment and non-discriminatory company, an increasingly tender area.

The manager of public and employee information is on the same management level as the manager of community relations, having twenty-seven persons under his supervision, as compared to twenty-four reporting to the manager of community relations. His work is supported by a supervisor of employee communication, with six publications supervisors and publications representatives who produce management bulletins on a regularized basis and publish employee magazines. Another section under this manager is that of the news bureau supervisor, who directs five news bureau representatives and a radio-television specialist.

A public affairs supervisor, reporting to the vice-president, performs substantially the same duties as the executive assistants, except that he and one assistant operate on a county and city political level, instead of the state. All are involved in the euphemistic area of government affairs which will be discussed in detail hereafter. In this particular company national government contact work is performed by a full-time consultant.

The public relations function is structured far more simply in the smaller company for relatively few people are involved, objectives are more limited, and programs far less complex in scope. The principles of operation remain the same, however, and eventually the same bases must be covered to one degree or another.

5

The Status Syndrome

THE LITERATURE of public relations is replete with the cries of its practitioners seeking a more intelligent understanding of their worth by management.

Of 1,200 responses received from members of the Public Relations Society of America, Inc. to a questionnaire soliciting topics for the annual convention discussion, 393 or 34.6 percent selected "How to Sell the Chief Executive on Public Relations." Next highest selection was "How to Research PR and Set Priorities," with 379 in favor. Thus, this vote in 1974 offered a poignant glimpse of what still fevers the public relations worker in every field — his lack of status.

With relation to the management charts in the American utility industry, the public relations function is a Joseph's coat of many colors. Nowhere does there appear to be uniformity. To some extent, the *size* of a company will frequently account for reporting relationships; certainly it will bear upon the numbers of personnel in a department and affect responsibilities and duties. Yet sometimes it is difficult to find rational answers for questions which occur when one examines various management charts. Nowhere was this oddity better exemplified than in the comprehensive public relations audit prepared for the American Gas Association in 1959.

It became my task to draft this first study ever undertaken to determine the public relations posture of a major segment of the utility industry. Titled, "Public Relations in the Gas Industry," the review followed and to some extent rested upon the findings of an Opinion Research Corporation survey of 1959, a nationwide sampling of public attitudes which pointed up the desirability of the industry's moving forward expeditiously and more expertly in the field of developing better relations with its various publics.

The factual basis for the audit hinged on results of a questionnaire sent to each privately owned gas utility company in the nation, requesting authoritative information on how public relations operated, where the function was placed on the management chart, the hierarchical rank of its leading personnel, its budgetary allotment compared to other functions, plus similar questions designed to determine just what prestige and authority it possessed in relation to other management tasks.

Although this 1959 analysis was concerned solely with gas companies, many conclusions apply to the electric and telephone industries as well since the public sometimes thinks of all utilities as a class. There is one minor caveat—historically, the electric utilities have been somewhat ahead of gas and telephone companies in sensing the moods of the public and becoming alert to the danger of public ownership.

Out of a total of 328 members of the American Gas Association questioned, 233 or 71 percent responded, accounting for 25,652,276 customer meters. This then represented about one-fourth of the nation's population and 92 percent of all gas customers. Included were both distributing and pipeline companies.

Out of the 233 companies, 101 (or slightly less than half) did not have public relations programs. These were smaller companies, representing only 2,719,143 meters. A heartening feature of the response was that those companies with PR programs served 90 percent of the gas customers of the country.

Up to this point, gas company public relations people rejoiced.

Then the picture changed. Of the 132 companies with programs, only 85 reported that the principal duty of their public relations manager was public relations. Others assigned "principal duties" to their managers as follows:

Press relations, 72; corporate management, 23; sales, 29; advertising, 58; employee relations, 22; customer relations, 30; community relations, 47; stockholder relations, 16. From this report, it became clear that public relations activities were something of a mishmash, with personnel, sales, and management tasks mixed into the job, and with an offbeat function emphasized to the detriment of some orthodox PR responsibility. Nor was it clear whether the advertising performed was corporate in nature, which belongs with public relations, or merchandising, which does not.

The questionnaire also disclosed that management relationships were scrambled. Although 89 public relations executives reported to the president, the requisite arrangement for effective operation, 17 were supervised by the executive vice-president, occasionally a tolerable proposal; 16 by the sales vice-president; 2 by the financial vice-president; 21 by sundry other vice-presidents undesignated by functional status, and 2 to a vice-president and secretary.

Then there were 2 by a director of sales and promotion; 4 by a general manager; 1 by a director of administration; 2 by a board of directors; 1 by the board chairman — certainly an exalted status for public relations — and one lone director of public relations was reportedly responsible to no one.

Of the 132 companies with programs, 41 evidently had so little confidence in either the function or its administrator that, when major policy or operating decisions were being considered, management declined to consult its public relations echelon.

There, simply, nearly twenty years ago, was the crux of the problem — lack of confidence by managment. On the other side, the public relations worker claims, with ample justification in certain cases, that he can not adequately perform because he is kept in the dark on matters within his administrative scope and expertise.

One is loath to suggest that avoidance of public relations counsel by management sometimes lies at the door of the PR function itself. This may indeed be the case, since a segment of utility management insists that two-plus-two always equals four, whereas in the often swiftly fluctuating realm of public opinion two-plus-two may equal four today, but five and maybe six tomorrow. This concept is sometimes most difficult to sell to management, trained in the world of precise and practical thinking.

It is this intangible aspect of public relations which baffles some members of utility management; and it is this "show me" skepticism that sets up a big hurdle for the public relations employee, who is usually in the middle or a lower box on the management chart, to surmount.

"How do you *know* that what you advise is right for this company at this time?" management asks the public relations executive who is certain of his position by experience and instinct. Unfortunately, he possesses no slide rule, no computer, no handy calculator to prove the verity of his position.

And so it is, when utilities public relations managers foregather to talk shop the discussion inevitably drifts around to status, along with the mistakes made by management that might easily have been avoided through consultation with the public relations cadre. There is certainly some meat in this coconut.

Yet, to be fair, it must be added that utilities management may counter such criticism by proclaiming that too many public relations employees have proved incapable of tendering sound advice. While downright incompetence may be to blame sometimes, the possibility remains that the employee's lowly status on the management chart has made him so timid and fearful of voicing convictions that he immediately assents to whatever the boss contemplates. Such a posture demolishes his usefulness as an advisor.

For three decades those engaged in public relations have striven for status and an influential niche in the hierarchy of utility industry management. Out of this struggle have come a few, relatively a very few, vice-presidencies, won by outstanding and talented individuals who clawed their way to the top deeply aware of what public relations can and cannot accomplish for public utilities.

With the passage of years the concept of the function is changing, sometimes for the better, and sometimes for the worse. Jack O'Dwyer, publisher of the *PR Newsletter*, speaking at the Publicity Club of Los Angeles, was quoted in the *Los Angeles Times* of May 8, 1972, as declaring that the term "public relations" has fallen into such disrepute that it "will probably wither from the lexicon in the 1970s."

O'Dwyer, the *Times* reported, "disdains efforts within the industry, notably by the Public Relations Society of America, to upgrade public relations to the status of a profession. It's not a profession. Personality, creativity, willingness to be different, guts, all count for more in PR than mastery of data."

Crisis of Confidence

He added that the drive to establish PR as a profession is led "by people in big corporations fighting for status, putting on airs. There's a lot of bitterness between this stuffy group and the workaday group."

By "workaday group" O'Dwyer was quite evidently referring to "publicists," who comprised his audience, resentful over being regarded as midwives rather than doctors. He went on to stress the importance of good press relations in his own understanding of effective public relations:

> *These PR executives are a prime reason for the anti-business climate that exists today because they can not personally go to the press—at which they have been looking down their noses all these years—and effectively plead their cases. These are guys who talk to the presidents of the biggest corporations but never—never—talk to the press. It's amazing.*

Also amazing and almost incomprehensible is that this ignorance exists in a quarter which should know better.

Objectively, despite all the vicissitudes, and particularly the difficulties inherent in proving its capacity to solve complex problems, the public relations of the utility industry has grown in stature over the years.

This has occurred because of the ability and training of strongly motivated men of integrity who have been willing to place their jobs on the line in urging courses of action and who ultimately proved the accuracy of their diagnosis and treatment of problems. Upon occasion utilities management has marveled at happy results achieved by application of public relations techniques and experience, and has expressed its appreciation with bigger pay checks and promotions. Ever so seldom this management gratitude has allowed a few—a very few—public relations executives to bask in the warm and pleasant confines of the inner circle where ultra-secret moves are contemplated, where grave decisions are debated and finally reached.

The drive by public relations personnel in the utilities field for upward mobility is not motivated solely by ego satisfaction. While not stated by those involved, their desire for status may really stem from realization of the need to be high enough on the organization chart to be taken seriously by senior management. In utilities, such managements resemble most of all the military table of organization. Who ever heard of a five-star general listening attentively to advice from a shavetail lieutenant or even a captain or major, when the shells are bursting?

So it is necessary that the function operate as a part of top management. In many corporations, the ideal arrangement has the vice-president of public relations reporting directly to the president. It is ideal because other executives are not so inclined to become recalcitrant over issues which can be swiftly met. In other companies, leaving title aside, the chief of public relations should have easy access to an executive who makes major corporate decisions. Such an executive should be temperamentally constituted to understand public relations in all its complex nuances. He should also have confidence in the intelligence, integrity, and competence of the public relations subordinate. Failing in this relationship, the function of public relations in a utility carries too heavy a burden. The result all too often will be shoddy performance, adding substance to the not infrequent criticism of those hard-nosed pragmatists who inhabit such departments as accounting, engineering, sales, financial, and legal.

6

Consultants: Should We, or Shouldn't We?

ONE OF THE impressive and enduring characteristics of the practice of corporate public relations—and especially that complex phase which specializes in utilities work—is the need for the functionally responsible executive to "talk it out" by reviewing options of a recommended course and considering prospective dangers.

The reason is clear: in executing a program of any complexity beyond the elementary no one can unequivocally predict a successful result. Here again the intangible obtrudes, for human nature, particularly that element involving the wellsprings of behavior and response, is notably irrational. Logic is one thing, emotions another, and what one man reveres, another may despise. If this were not the case, Freud's disciples would long since have been out of business.

Perhaps one of the most illuminating examples of this tendency of the human animal to aberrant behavior has been sketched by O. Henry in one of his short stories. Two men confronting the prospective dissolution of their marriages recount how each would react if abandoned by his spouse. One said he would certainly end his life, being unable to continue without his loved one; the other insisted that he was made of sterner stuff and would confront the loss with the quiet resignation of an Indian mystic. The O. Henry twist lay in reversing the roles of the protagonists when the blows fell: the actions of each were exactly contrary to prediction.

No matter how clearly the public relations expert may conceptualize the possible result of an undertaking, he can never be *certain*. Hovering over every major project, with any pretense to complexity, lies an air of *uncertainty*, the iffy factor that pragmatic generalists find so objectionable and frustrating.

"Will it play in Peoria?" a former President's men were wont to ask, applying this cynical litmus test to a project's feasibility.

Will it work, supervising executives inquire in reviewing a public relations plan that depends upon specific and favorable acceptance by either the public or their representatives. It should be noted that the inclusive designation, public, portrays persons of indescribably diverse opinions, prejudices, ages, backgrounds, education, wants, status, and ethnic origins, to say nothing of political persuasions.

Because of the unpredictability of a project's ultimate success, and because no individual (however experienced or perceptive) is competent to consider all eventualities attending a course of conduct, or unerringly prophesy result, utilities have long deemed it desirable to undertake one and sometimes two preliminary steps before hazarding commitment to a plan.

First will come staff review and discussion. Here, in frank interplay of co-workers' opinion, is the initial opportunity to examine a given idea (an important requirement in determining the merit of a position), spot weaknesses, provide suggestions for alteration, or even pronounce a valedictory.

These sessions resemble those of the popular brainstorming type indulged in by other executives, usually off premises at a pleasant spa, where refreshments are plentiful and everything is on the expense account. Nevertheless, the give and take of the utility PR meeting is unrelieved by any semblance of levity, being solely devoted to seeking flaws in the concept. Staff members are afloat in the same boat as their superior and fully aware they will likely swim or sink with him, depending on how their craft survives the volleys of critical grapeshot from executive rivals or, even more dicey, whether their proposal makes sense when it is ultimately presented to the chief, be he executive vice-president, president, or chairman of the board.

Even the lowliest staff member has been known to volunteer something of import as everyone scrutinizes every detail of the enterprise proposed. Participants in this appraisal or forum for the interchange of ideas have likened it to "bouncing a ball against the wall."

Another preliminary measure which can help ensure success is use of an outside public relations counsel or consultant. This practice is becoming more common among utilities, but it is not always flattering either to the competency or status of the public relations chief. Even so, he may welcome such outside help for several reasons. On the one hand, it tends to dilute responsibility in the event of failure, a not unwelcome consideration. On the other, he has probably gained for his point of view an articulate and prestigious ally, bound to him by professional *esprit de corps*. Most important, he has probably enhanced the chances of a successful program.

In practice, the terms counsel and consultant are often synonymous and used interchangeably. To the purist there may be differences. The counsel serves mainly as a competent advisor, often on a long-term basis and compensated by a stipulated, regularized fee. He attends staff conferences, meets frequently with his client, and is continuously available for discussion. He is prepared to perform writing tasks or production chores in his own office. He is a confidant of his client and, if necessary, a salesman to top management on behalf of his client. He often serves as the "wall" the ball strikes. He should be, and usually is, an experienced, literate, and protean individual. To his work he brings an outside and presumably objective viewpoint, even though it can become slightly tainted at times by close association with his client and their mutually sympathetic bond. Out of this rapport there may grow a tendency for counsel and client to think alike and ultimately embrace similar conclusions.

In contrast, the consultant may operate chiefly as an oracle. It is he to whom the baffled PR executive may turn when confronting a puzzle without any ready solution or to which all solutions seem to carry with them dangerous consequences. The consultant, with recognized expertise, is presumably equipped to suggest new and broad dimensions to any program contemplated. He is expected to guide an undertaking safely through storms of counterattack, and avoid a dangerous, inept performance. Like the counsel, he too, being one of the brotherhood of the bedevilled, will strive mightily to support his company colleague—*up to a point.*

His loyalty, however, is divided because his charter of

employment may be broadened to include contact with corporate authority above and beyond that of the responsible public relations executive. When this is the case, he risks being caught between the Scylla of professional allegiance and the Charybdis of concern over making a mistake in the eyes of top management.

However, most consultants rarely experience any difficulty in harmonizing what might seem a dilemma since, as everyone knows, words are not necessarily explicitly expressive. What with discussion and repetition, positions that may initially appear to be hard and fast tend to erode with the passage of time. In the end, if a maneuver fails, as many do, the responsibility is mutually shared.

Unlike the counsel whose work for a corporation may be on a continuing basis from month to month or year to year, a consultant may be summoned intermittently depending upon need. Whatever the company commitment regarding employment status, and recognizing that counsel and consultant are used synonymously, this fresh and independent viewpoint is usually beneficial.

There are certain tests for the selection of a PR advisor:

Is he qualified by accomplishment and experience?

Does his past professional record indicate that he has functioned with independence and integrity?

Is he personally agreeable, that is, will he foster pleasant relationships with company executives, despite honest differences of opinion? Or, on the other hand, does his manner reflect an abrasive hubris?

Will he vigorously support a point of view in the face of supervising executive disagreement? Or will he weakly fold, because outranked?

The last point is crucial, for the introduction into a company of an expert voice to be relied upon in event of emergency can only be supported if there is no trimming, no modification of position, no retreat to the expedient when a final judgment is solicited.

Such a voice, unrestrained by any need of appeasing a hierarchical superior having the power to recommend salary increases, can be of effective assistance not only to the public relations department but to the company.

When Kipling reported there are nine and sixty ways of constructing tribal lays "and every single one of them is right," he might with justice have said the same about most public relations programs. Variability of approach is their hallmark, an unhappy circumstance duly noted by detractors who argue that the occupation lacks established disciplines. This is untrue, of course, for there are the rigorous delineation of objectives, the opinion surveys, the analyses of methods, the testing of results, all more or less inviolate methodology. Many alluring pathways may beckon toward the ultimate goal, and it is here that the objective and unfettered analyst from the outside may earn his prescribed fee by pointing to the right one.

Planning
for
Rate Increases

7

Prelude to Planning

GEORGE SANTAYANA once warned that if we disregard history we are condemned to relive it.

On June 5, 1952, the *Public Utilities Fortnightly* published my allusions to the financial problems of utilities:

The pattern is broad and contains many colors, but here are a few of the threads:

1. The constant cheapening of the dollar through inflation, resulting in depressing the living standards of large segments of the population.

2. The growing burden of the tax load which requires utilities to request $2.20 in gross increase for every dollar of net revenue. This, coupled with loss of dollar value, has spurred ratepayers to ever more militant resistance to rate increases which cause,

> *(a) Regulatory bodies to authorize net returns which tend toward lower areas of the 'zone of reasonableness' resulting in*

3. Repetitive rate increase applications due to the utilities experiencing

> *(a) Constant labor, price, and tax increases;*
>
> *(b) Serious time lags involved in the 'due process' functioning of the regulatory process;*
>
> *(c) A rapid 'slippage' downward of net earnings caused by*

*failure of regulatory bodies to grant sufficiently adequate relief
in the first place.*

*4. Failure of most–perhaps all–of the major utilities to recognize
clearly at the beginning of the inflationary binge that the problem
posed by higher rates and higher return was essentially as much a
public relations problem as a legal one, and, finally*

*5. This inability of the utilities to come to grips with the public
relations challenge facing them, which left both the utilities and
the regulatory bodies at the mercy of every articulate pressure
group (of which there are many) and inevitably required the
regulators to think in terms of narrowed earnings.*

And a few paragraphs later: *The investor is beginning to take
his savings elsewhere for investment.*

One ponders these comments of more than two decades ago
and has the uncanny feeling of having walked through a revolving
door. If there has been any change at all, that change has been for
the worse. Utility rates are still in disarray. Regulatory lag has not
only been disappointing, it has been scandalous. Consumers not
only bitterly protest at rate hearings, they march, carrying placards.
Sam Shulsky, widely read syndicated financial columnist, observed in the *Los Angeles Herald-Examiner* of July 30, 1974, that the
omission of a dividend by Consolidated Edison on its common
stock "yanked utilities investments into a new era as violently as
Hiroshima marked the beginning of a new atomic age." Shulsky
continued: "The utility industry has entered a new era and faces a
set of problems from the investor's point of view and, most
certainly—and concurrently—from the point of view of the utility
customer. Cheap power is on the way out and there is no point to
look for its return until fuel and money and tax costs are reduced.
And that will be—as the kids used to say—'after never.' " (Shulsky
might also have mentioned escalating labor and materials costs.)

As though to emphasize Shulsky's remarks, and carry them to
their logical conclusion, W.R. van Liew, vice-president of Fitch
Investors, billed as an expert in the utilities field, observed in a
column published in the "OTC Market Chronicle" in the same
issue of the *Herald-Examiner* as Mr. Shulsky's article:

*The days of utility service being a 'bargain basement item' are
gone. With rising operating costs and rising taxes at the local
levels, the cost of utility service, direct as well as indirect . . . is*

almost certain to continue increasing over the long term. Thus the consumer is entering a relatively new era of cost levels . . . Soon or later he may be forced to adopt a totally new concept of relating the cost of a utility service not to a price which existed at one time, but to the value of the service . . . How valuable is it to have light, heat, communications, and the necessities and conveniences in the home . . .? Are these utility services as valuable to the consumer as, for example, food, shelter, or even gasoline? Can the consumer adopt a 'willingness' to pay for a utility service . . .? Actually the consumer has never been tested fully in this respect . . . The consumer's attitude is critical to the industry . . . If the consumer has understanding, an acceptance of higher rates is possible, provided the service is good . . . Until recently, the treatment of the consumer from the standpoint of taking him into the confidence of the company and/or the regulator has left something to be desired.

Mr. van Liew felt action must be taken to win consumer understanding and possibly acceptance of a continuously rising rate structure—adding that "the financial viability of the industry is derived from the pocketbook of the consumer."

One must plead indulgence for quoting so liberally from both Shulsky and van Liew, but public relations reasoning, often necessarily empirical in concept, has frequently offered conclusions causing cynical utilities executives to raise the cry of "Wolf, wolf," in disbelief.

Today, these are perilous times in which to cry "Wolf" or to suspect that the warnings of public relations practitioners are self-serving and designed to enhance status. To do so in this period might be akin to Caesar scoffing at the soothsayer's forebodings on his way to the Forum, or to the captain of the *Titanic* reprimanding a seaman for suggesting that icebergs might lie ahead.

For the ineluctable fact is that Shulsky, van Liew, and others have hit the nail squarely on the head when they write about the necessity for utilities to seek ever higher rates and the consumer to pay them, even while his standard of living is being driven down in many other ways by higher prices of food, clothing, and shelter.

The further fact is that even in the best of times obtaining compensatory rates under regulation has never been easy for utilities. The task itself comprises a constant, never ending problem. It rides the backs of public utilities like an Old Man of the Sea, accoutred with boots and spurs. It requires batteries of staff attorneys, as well as outside counsel. It requires engineers, accountants, specialists in fuel supply, in equipment design and underground storage. Most of all it requires a professionally planned and executed public relations program—not on the day the rate application is filed but before, sometimes long before.

This is what Mr. van Liew had in mind when he referred to winning customer understanding of the need for ever higher rates, and this is the area where virtually every utility has done less than a satisfactory job. In most cases the result has been certain: regulatory bodies and their appointing powers, politically conscious of adverse public opinion and how it might be reflected at the next election, have more often than not cringed whenever authorizing increases.

In offering his recommendations, Mr. van Liew was quite evidently writing from the common sense viewpoint of a security analyst. He might be both comforted and flattered to know that the Opinion Research Corporation, through scientific opinion sampling, long ago reported that familiarity of the public with a company and an understanding of its problems leads to acceptance, and a company well liked and trusted by the public may increase its rates with far less adverse public reaction than one disliked and distrusted.

The time has truly arrived when public utilities must refurbish and reevaluate management thinking on public relations efforts that can determine success or failure in the area of fair return based upon compensatory rates.

This will be a difficult chore, at best, not because the task is either herculean or of Byzantine complexity, but mainly because it demands planning and action far in advance of a rate filing, the unification of effort which welds all interested company departments together for the attainment of a specific goal, centralized control of action, with particular emphasis upon the legal, rate, engineering, and public relations phases of the undertaking.

8

Inflation and Fair Rates

OBLIGATED under their monopolistic franchises to provide service on demand, utilities have been ground between the upper millstone of burgeoning costs with attendant shortage of supply, and the lower millstone of prices fixed by government fiat.

High interest rates, roadblocks to construction by ecologists, ever-increasing wage rates, a demoralized equity market inhibiting them from common stock sales, a general tightening of credit, an unstable political picture at all levels, the rise of consumerism rooted in bitter resentment over prices—all these have profoundly affected the viability of utilities.

One recourse is to seek long term lines of credit at heavy cost. The other is—hopefully—to raise rates, and it is this avenue for relief that has catapulted them into the twin domains of political and public attitudes, the two tied together by the umbilical cord of self-interest.

In authorizing higher rates during inflation the politician is animated by the fear of possible consequences from an aroused citizenry at the ballot box. In its turn, the public is aware of this fear and applies pressure where it will do the most good, on the politician responsible for signing the rate decision.

In order to obtain compensatory rates, or at least move in that direction, since during inflation a fair return lasts just so long, the utility must address itself to political and public opinion.

The first question utility management must ask itself before filing a rate application is: in the past, how well has the utility met its responsibility of winning political and public goodwill and understanding of its problems? On the answer to this question the ultimate liberality of a regulatory agency may depend.

One very large utility may be a classic case in point.

In August, 1968, the *Wall Street Journal* carried a page one, column one story, with the heading: "Unhappy Utility — Bad Image — Bloated Work Force Balk [name of utility] Progress — New Chairman Retires Aging Executives, Trims Costs, Defends High Power Rates." And the next line in the heading: "Did Contractors Rig Bids?" The story went on to castigate the utility's service and its treatment of customer complaints.

In early 1974—some six years later—this utility sent a shock through investment circles by passing its dividend, and utility stocks throughout the United States promptly tumbled in price. Here is a perfect example of a utility failing to meet its commitment to the consuming public, with the inevitable result that it could not obtain a fair return on the stockholders' investment.

So, in a utility's effort to be successful in obtaining fair rates, rates which will provide for depreciation, cost of service, and a reasonable net, it must be assumed that the utility offers prompt, dependable, and courteous service.*

With service assumed, and provided that all legal and financial presentations are expertly prepared, what steps of a public relations nature should be undertaken by a utility in seeking rate relief?

Upon cessation of World War II, the State of California witnessed a rash of substantial utility rate increases. Coming after prewar decreases and a wartime price freeze, these proved shocking to consumers and brought a spate of newspaper scare headlines.

Evincing concern over public repercussions and consequent resistance, then Governor Earl Warren summoned to his guber-

---

*Importance of a company's behavior is shown graphically by Pacific Telephone's examination of customer attitudes, undertaken in April, 1967, and published under the title: "How Customer Attitudes Are Really Determined." The analysis showed that *nine times out of ten*, unfavorable attitudes toward the company are the result of unfavorable experiences by customers. About half of the unfavorable experiences were *service related*, one-third cost related, and the remainder of a general company nature.

natorial sanctum the president of the California Public Utilities Commission, his appointee.

Why, asked the Governor, *do the utilities and the Commission figuratively hit the consumer over the head and out-of-the-blue with a sudden and heavy increase in his utility bills, admitting that such increases are required? You should foreshadow the necessity for higher rates, long before the application is filed, and this is a task for the utility. Such a preliminary preparation of public opinion will go a long way toward avoiding public surprise and shock. The program will provide public understanding, and acceptance.* *

The idea born at that time in the mind of one of the shrewdest politicians of our era was immediately adopted by California utilities and has been followed since as an integral part of the pattern supporting the need for new and higher rates.

Looking backward, the governor's suggestion was so simple, yet so psychologically sound in terms of public opinion and acceptance, that today it appears astonishing no one responsible for coping with consumer attitudes had thought of it earlier.

Before the gubernatorial suggestion, the procedures for seeking higher rates were swift, uncomplicated, and perfunctory.

The practice was extremely simple and particularly unrewarding from the standpoint of public relationships. The utility, deciding it required higher rates, had its legal department draft a formal application, couched in almost incomprehensible legalistic and financial jargon, with those points which might affect a bill paying customer well hidden in the wilderness of verbiage. Being a public record as soon as filed, a copy of the application was placed in the Commission "press basket," subject to scrutiny by media representatives once an hour, sometimes more frequently. Whereupon the reporters—challenged by the obscurity of language and suspecting an attempt to conceal information—would pounce upon the Commission press officer and other staff members, demar ﹖ clarification. The obvious result: usually major emphasis on ﹖ application by the press and other media.

*While the quotation may not express the exact words of the Governor, it gives a true representation of his views, as related by the Commission president to the writer, then Commission Director of Public Relations.

Planning for Rate Increases

From that point on, until the Commission decision, there was little if any news coverage. Of course, when the decision was issued containing information on the additonal gross revenues allowed the applicant on an annual basis, news interest suddenly revived, often in a startling manner with scareheads. The ratepaying public fumed, firing off protesting letters and telegrams to both elected and appointive officials. Clearly, these are the factors Governor Warren had in mind when he decided to search for a remedy.

Today, the more sophisticated utilities undertake a carefully planned and ably prosecuted campaign of preconditioning the official and the customer mind, a low key "selling" of necessity.

It begins as early as the finance officer of the company can determine that, upon a future date, the utility will require rate relief. At that point, it comprises a hint only, a possibility to be mentioned publicly in many forums and through various channels, speeches by executives, financial interviews, plant tours, employee bulletins, notes to various management levels. It is a tiny cloud no larger than a hand upon the financial horizon—but as time passes it grows, is seen more clearly—and then, at the proper moment in the judgment of the public relations officer, the information effort begins. That "proper moment" is largely determined by how long it will take to brief the key officials and public opinion makers before it is practically necessary to file the application for higher rates.

9

Rates—and the Agency

TODAY, the rate problem for all utilities is nothing less than appalling.

As a striking example, early in 1975 a single natural gas utility filed two applications with the state regulatory agency for rate increases totaling $690,741,000, planned to be applied over a period of seven years.

A report of National Services, Inc., of New York, a utility rate analysts group, publicized by the Associated Press in September, 1974, describes the proportions of the problem.

During the first six months of 1974, industrial and commercial rates charged by the nation's largest utilities rose an average of 55.4 percent above a similar period in 1973, while similar rates in 1973 rose only 12.4 percent above the 1972 level.

The survey noted that Florida Power Corp. of St. Petersburg, Florida, posted the highest increase, 89 percent in the first six months of 1974 over a like period in 1973. Others for the same periods: Long Island Lighting Company, 87.6 percent; New Jersey Public Service Electric and Gas Company, 76 percent; Southern California Edison Company, 72 percent; Baltimore Gas and Electric Company, 63.8 percent; Philadelphia Electric Company, 63.6 percent; and New York's Consolidated Edison Company, 43 percent.

Following publication of the report, Southern California Edison Company claimed figures for that company were inaccurate, stating that actual increases in the first half of 1974 averaged 25 percent, with residential rates up 23 percent, and industrial rates up 29 percent. For the 12 months between June, 1973, and June, 1974, Edison said, residential rates rose 35 percent, while industrial rates climbed 66 percent.

Amid customer cries of unfair and excessive pricing, a number of other utilities, as well as some of those cited, reported that heavier increases were required. Newspaper editorial pages in Southern California Edison's territory, for one, were deluged in the closing months of 1974 with letters from complaining ratepayers, accusing the utility of earning swollen profits. Examples from two such letters appearing September 24, 1974, in the *Desert Sun* of Palm Springs, California:

> . . .*but it seems to me that something is missing—that is, the company's profit picture. According to the August 10, 1974, issue of* Business Week *magazine, Southern California Edison realized a profit of $105.2 million during the first six months of 1974, reflecting an increase of a whopping 76 percent over the same period of 1973.* From another letter, same newspaper, same day: *Thus, what is a fair return? What can be done to reduce SCE's charges? What can be done to make it possible to afford electricity? Would like to suggest that your newspaper request an open hearing in Palm Springs council chambers immediately . . . It is not right that they be allowed to continue to exploit their monopolistic position and add to the economic trauma of the country.*

While there may be some relaxation of the strangling grip which forces thus far uncontrollable exert upon the economy, although one can not imagine how, a relaxation would probably provide only a temporary alleviation, not a permanent cure. New and higher price plateaus have been frozen into the economy, while economists, most of whom have displayed notable talents for both disagreeing and guessing, talk in terms of various solutions requiring years for implementation. The best they have managed until now is to prescribe placebos for a patient whose fever continues to rise.

Enmeshed in the need for unprecedented rate increases, while millions subsist on unemployment insurance and the dole, the utilities may have signally failed to delineate clearly for the public the awesome proportions of the problem.

There have been fragmented references to it, of course. The media have not failed to emblazon information on rate filings, particularly specifying the gross dollar amounts sought, but nowhere has the gravity of the rate issue been frankly explained with a gloves-off, no-holds-barred, here-are-the-facts approach. Not yet has the dark and ominous picture been painted in its entirety for the consuming public.

True, there have been toe-in-the-water reports that fuel costs are high and going higher, and that rates must follow; that construction of badly needed plant has been deferred or abandoned totally; that hoped-for nuclear power is being balked by the attacks of ecologists; that natural gas is being sought diligently in faraway places, and hence must cost more at the burner tip.

Nevertheless, the dimensions of the impact of cataclysmic forces on American utilities, *if present trends continue without change*, have not yet been publicly acknowledged or, in a sense, shouted from the housetops.

The narrower necessity for the beleaguered utility must have three objectives:

1. To develop and maintain as best it can a quiescent public acceptance of its rate necessities.
2. To obtain compensatory rates from the regulatory agency.
3. To obtain rate decisions *expeditiously*.

The final point is paramount, since some regulatory agencies have evinced a proclivity for foot-dragging on decisions, presumably petrified by a fear of public—which means political—repercussions. While not defensible, such inordinate delays are understandable, for although regulators thoroughly enjoy *reducing* rates, few have the stomach for braving the public wrath so often attendant on *raising* rates, especially in a recession and inflationary period.

This being the case, the earliest information on the necessity for a rate filing should be provided the president or chairman of the regulatory agency having jurisdiction, plus other agency members. If intra-agency relationships of its members are cordial, it is probable that the presiding official will undertake the task of informing his colleagues of what portends, but if members are split on ideological or personal grounds (quite frequently the situation), then members must be contacted and informed individually.

The supposition here is that the utility has kept its political house in order by timely meetings with regulatory agency voting members, such visitations occurring *when nothing whatever is sought from these public officials.*

This is a sensitive point with some regulators, who have been known to complain:

I only see utilities executives when they want something. It would seem to me that we have a basic, definite mutuality of interest—I, of course, representing the public, utility management representing the stockholders. Still, in a broad sense, we both represent the public interest *for our responsibilities are inextricably intertwined, to such an extent that they blur and merge.*

*It is my job to assure the public of good and reliable service at reasonable rates—and at the same time assure the shareholder of a reasonable return on the property he has dedicated to public use. The task of management is identical. We both must keep well abreast of current public utility problems. So don't wait to see me until your house is on fire and you need help.*Come when you want nothing, *and thus keep me continuously posted on your current undertakings.*

Sophisticated utilities executives long ago learned the lesson of becoming personally acquainted with regulatory commissioners, and they also have learned that certain perils exist in these relationships. They may preliminarily brief the public official on the facts, allowing the urgency of need to speak for itself, but sometimes it is dangerous to become too persuasive before formally filing for rate relief. There is always grave hazard in talking to an official on the subject of a filing after submission, while the case is being heard, and before decision. Most utility executives, not all, are properly wary of such *ex parte* contacts, for overstepping the bounds of both law and good judgment can bring seriously adverse results.

Historically, one of the nagging problems for utilities has been that of regulatory lag. Repeated efforts have been undertaken by several agencies to slay this dragon of delay with varying degrees of success. The major difficulty lies in the complexities of the rate fixing process itself: the necessity for staff examination; the burdensome engineering, accounting, and legal review; the requirements for notifications; the concern by the agency for consumer protests and for due process.

In normal times, lag, while always frustrating, may be endurable, rarely wreaking havoc with a company's financial structure. However, in a double-digit inflationary period it can become unendurable and oppressive.

One expedient is to suggest temporary rates subject to later adjudication and possible refund. Such rates, if authorized, tend to relieve the continuous pressure on utility costs, while rates fixed a year after filing are rendered obsolete by the never-ceasing push of inflationary prices.*

An almost unbelievable example of regulatory lag is that of a major California utility which received rate relief *eighteen months after applying*, requiring the affected company to announce, on the very day of the decision, that it would reluctantly be forced to file again immediately because financial attrition had dissipated whatever benefits might accrue from the new rates. In this particular case, the decision was not only extraordinarily late in coming, its findings had drastically reduced the company's stated need in terms of annual gross revenues, a second blow.

To circumvent similar treatment by the agency in the future, a leading utility in the same state and under the same jurisdiction publicly announced it planned to file for new and higher rates *to become effective twelve to eighteen months later*.

---

*Under the Natural Gas Act, the Federal Power Commission may authorize higher interstate gas rates, subject to refund. Some states may do the same under state statutes.

10

The Position Paper

ONE OF THE difficulties a utility confronts in assuming a public position is speaking with one voice. The same handicap burdens government and corporations generally. However, in all cases where it becomes necessary to provide information for the public, nothing may equal in importance the necessity for telling the same story in the same way. In the highest levels of government, cabinet officers have been fired for talking out of a different side of their mouths than their President. General MacArthur's example comes readily to mind as a willful violator of the party line. For his temerity he was sacked by President Truman.

In private industry and particularly in public utilities, similar offenses rarely exact such draconian reprisal by management, where derelictions in the informational sector are usually tolerantly regarded as probably due to the inherent stupidity of the perpetrator. He may be blocked for promotion, at least temporarily, and he may be reprimanded, but unless his indiscretion was of monumental proportion, he will not be cast into the cold.

Yet in order to avoid, as far as humanly possible, judgmental errors and lapses of memory by executives, something was needed by public relations directors charged with informational responsibilities and unwilling to risk criticism for disseminating *misinformation*.

This necessity mothered the position paper, a careful, precise, detailed, and factual memorandum, giving a step-by-step recital of all the information required by anyone within the company who discusses the issue with any outsider, and designed to answer every legitimate question as well as some illegitimate ones.

The position paper has varied uses in the utility field. Why is a rate increase being sought? What prompts the need for a nuclear power plant? How does efficiency serve the public interest? What are the arguments against the public ownership of any specific utility—electric, gas, water, telephone, or transportation—although almost all urban transit lines are now either publicly owned or publicly subsidized.

Perhaps the most commonly used and critically important précis created by the public relations department of a utility relates to the filing for rate relief with a regulatory body. It is pointed to answering two questions: first, why is it necessary to seek higher rates? second, if authorized, what would the projected increase mean to the *average* customer in terms of his monthly bill?

In order to minimize impact on the individual customer, it has been routine for utility publicists to "bury" the total annual revenue dollar amount sought and, instead, feature the *monthly average* increase per *average* individual consumer. This helps in avoiding scare headlines in the press proclaiming millions of dollars of increase, and is achieved easily by dividing the dollars by what are sometimes millions of ratepayers, and quoting average usages. By this accounting technique the company informs the public that monthly billings will increase by "64 cents per month for the average customer," or "8 cents," "10 cents," or similar miniscule amounts.

In recent years there have been many major reasons for a succession of utility rate increase requests, among them increases in wages and benefits for employees. It was only a few years ago that 5 percent wage increases were sought by employees; today workers represented by unions demand anywhere from 11 percent to as high as they believe the traffic is likely to bear. It has become one of the curious facets of employee-management relationships in the utility industry that there is a tacit assumption by *both* that each year *there will be a wage increase*, with the amount and fringe benefits subject to negotiation. This is a country mile away from the period when no such assumption existed by either side. The result has been unstable rates pressured upward, causing public criticism of the utility and the regulatory agency.

Fringe benefits now available in the utility industry are too numerous to list, ranging all the way from the orthodox medical, to dental services, paid life insurance, plus ever earlier retirements, although the latter are funded, it must be confessed, in some companies by pensions rather niggardly when compared to other industries and downright penurious if contrasted to those furnished by taxpayers to their public servants.

Other segments of private enterprise facing rising employee demands, while bitter about capitulating to what sometimes amounts to brigandage enforced by strikes, can pass on to the ultimate buyer the higher costs involved. Not so with the utility, which enjoys no easy pass along privilege. The utility must appeal to government for the right to raise the price of its product, and the public relations representative of the utility must use his best efforts to sell the need for higher rates. Here the mild or the violent attitude of the public influences the regulatory agency. Therefore, the public relations task is pointed toward the preconditioning of the public and the official mind in order to avoid opposition, which is likely to reflect itself in anti-increase editorials in the media, and subsequent appearance by protestors and/or their attorneys at agency public hearings on the application.

There are other substantial reasons why the utility seeks financial relief during the worst inflation in history: costs of borrowing money, costs of materials and supplies, costs of new plant construction to provide service, costs of the worldwide search for low sulfur fuel oil, or natural gas. Unless higher monthly revenues from the customers are mandated, the utility cannot function in the role assigned to it by custom and legislation. This is in sharp contrast to the free will the consumer exercises in other aspects of his relationship to the market, where he can buy, or not buy, or defer a purchase, according to his election.

It becomes the task of the utility public relations echelon to describe in easily understandable terms the revenue requirements and relate those utility needs to the life experience of the customer and other special groups: city attorneys, city councilmen, county supervisors, state assemblymen, and senators; opinion molders of every complexion, such as newspaper editors, chamber of commerce officers and members, service clubs personnel, and citizen leaders generally.

Nor must employees of the utility itself be overlooked. They have often been characterized as the first line in carrying information on the necessity for a rate increase to friends, neighbors, and relatives. As a matter of fact employees are natural allies of a company on every public issue. The role of retired employees in company activities is a subject for later discussion.

The question of who should prepare the company position paper on a major issue sometimes becomes a subject of departmental dispute with legal, financial, occasionally engineering, and always (hopefully) public relations involved. Preference here should always be accorded public relations which, presumably, is equipped by experience to couch its language in comprehensible terms for the layman. Other departments, quite naturally, have a tendency to lapse into the jargons of their professional disciplines.

Once agreement is reached on exposition of the company's position, it becomes necessary to develop the program and communicate it to the various groups.

These may be categorized as: community leaders, government officials, the general public, employees, and stockholders.

The initial approach should be low key, the utility public relations department hoping that the public and officialdom will receive the information in the same manner. If, however, the informational effort arouses opposition, the department must be geared to respond by intensifying its efforts and broadening its techniques.

Leaders in the communities should be visited by division representatives who, over the years, may be presumed to have cultivated friendships at the local level. Here, support for a company proposal should be solicited but, if unobtainable, the fallback strategy must be to attempt to mute opposition.

Before undertaking their community calls, division employees should meet with public relations personnel and be supplied with copies of the approved statement of position, containing the factual material, which is left as a giveaway piece with those visited.

Similar contacts are made with public officials from the governor down to the city council level, and with editors and editorial writers.

To guard against articulate opposition from the public or officials, it is customary to commission a utility's advertising agency to prepare a series of advertisements to be published on a standby basis if deemed necessary by a darkening public opinion climate. Stuffers for company bills are also prepared against their possible need.

Along with these steps go meetings of all employees, where they are fully informed of the company's program. Full information is additionally provided in all the company's internal publications.

One company vice-president summed up his program in this way:

"We develop our position paper as a clear, concise, and truthful recital of the utility position. At the same time, we maintain a flexible posture in all our activities so that we may meet any untoward conditions that may arise."

A time-tested stratagem for muffling incipient opposition to a planned, necessary move is to identify the company's interest with that of the public, and in cases of utilities' needs today no element of deception attaches to this ploy. The *Los Angeles Herald-Examiner*, in an editorial of October 23, 1974, clearly enunciated the theme of mutual responsibility, "Utilities' Plight Also the Public's."

After describing the revenue requirements of utilities in the present period, the newspaper continued:

We're not suggesting that the public start loving the utilities. They may find themselves looked upon even more coldly as they continue to pass through their higher costs of oil, natural gas, coal, and labor. But the public should be aware that the utilities have a big problem, and it's the public's problem, too.

The editorial might reasonably have emphasized that the problem is not necessarily a *local* one, and hence no particular city, county, or state may consider itself aggrieved, as emphasized in advertising run by the national organization of electric power companies.

These utilities, in *Time* magazine, November 4, 1974, assured ratepayers in a full page message: "Electric rates are going up just about everywhere." The ad continued: "They have to. The inflationary spiral is affecting the costs of all goods and services, including the costs of making electricity." Further on: "Although we continue to find more efficient ways of doing things, the cost of electricity, like everything else, is going up *wherever* you live." (Emphasis in original.)

The warning is clear: there can be no escape for anyone from the pressure of rising costs and increased rates.

11

Hello, Comrade!

THEY STROLL the hard, marbled corridors of the Rayburn Building, and the Old and New Senate office buildings, wandering from office to office, outwardly relaxed, sometimes like policemen walking their beats—seemingly serene and composed, their faces bland, frequently smiling, always friendly. Their eyes, even when they smile, are bleakly intent like those of a prize dog coming to point.

They purvey personality more often than they provide campaign contributions. Their warm, standardized salutation to congressmen, senators, and associates, or on a lower level to state-elected officials and city councilmen, is "Hello, Comrade," a cheery, "all's well with the world" greeting but, more important, a significant presumption that here there exists a bond, a mutuality of interest, unspoken but tacitly understood.

They want to be liked, for being liked is their merchandise, their stock in trade, the totality of what they have to sell to an employer. They are "legislative advocates"—a kindly and pretentious euphemism for lobbyists, and sometimes their business cards carry the designation "public relations," which is difficult for many public relations professionals to take.

Full-time lobbying is a far cry from the practice of public relations. It is contact work of a high order—the transmission and selling of ideas and a point of view, a building of personal friend-

Crisis of Confidence

ships seemingly noncommercial, requiring the inborn and acquired skill of a psychologist, the innate sensitivity of a violin virtuoso and, at times, the thick hide of a rhinoceros when compelled to barge in aggressively on behalf of a client.

Even so, these attributes are commendable, and while the tasks performed by the lobbyist may not be classified by the purist as constituting public relations, they are certainly of vital importance to the utility or any company dedicated to the welfare of its customers, its stockholders, and its employees.

It is a platitude to suggest that government now permeates our lives, and nowhere is this more evident than in the operation of the public utility. At times the analyst is hard pressed to discern where private management ends and government begins, and sometimes the legions of attorneys now staffing utilities are themselves baffled in trying to determine the difference between the two, for theory is one thing, substance another. The fact is that public utilities live and prosper, or wither and die, almost at the whim of public agencies of one level or another. These agencies, as well as the political superiors who appoint and influence them, are composed of men, subject to all the human strengths and frailties.

Thus the lobbyist is important as one element in the mosaic of the utility's relationships with its several publics. In a sense, he may be compared to a sword with a cutting edge—needed on occasion but always subject to the careful control of a *knowledgable superior*, who should be a skilled public relations executive, not a general management executive.

Some lobbyists on their own may cause incalculable mischief, as witness the Dita Beard memorandum, bringing in its wake a whole series of evil consequences for I. T. & T., her employer. From the record, it appears that she reported to the company's chief executive and, if so, this might be accounted the root cause of her blunder.

For in many cases, business chief executives are incredibly naive when confronting the (to them) Alice in Wonderland world of politics, so often clouded by the necessity for small evasions, chicanery, and, upon occasion, outright lying. In the main, the conduct of a utility—as well as other modern business—is grounded upon integrity, of honest dealing man to man, where one's word, once given, may not be violated. Not all politicians operate in this milieu. Theirs is an environment where survival is paramount to all else. It is the dominant theme of their existence as officeholders; to this all else must be subordinated. This is not to say that business executives are not attuned to the fang and claw aspects of the corporate jungle, both internal and external. It is certainly not to say that all corporations are kindly do-gooders when grappling for markets or mergers—for such excursions exhibit shark-like tendencies, as well as Machiavellian deception. It is simply to say that, taken as individuals, the great majority of business executives are decent, honorable men, attached to telling the truth, even though it hurts, and as gullible as Simple Simon in the political arena. How else explain the illegal corporate contributions from businessmen in the Watergate mess, save upon the grounds of an almost incomprehensible naivete, coupled with fear?

No public relations executive worth his salt would have recommended to his management that a corporate contribution be made to Nixon reelection agent Maurice Stans secretly and in violation of law, because one of the cardinal elements of the proper practice of public relations is truth and a profound respect for the public interest—at least the public interest as it appears to the eye of the beholder. But a cynical lobbyist, whose credo, like that of some politicians, is to succeed at any cost, may have.

The point is that, in the main, the lobbyist can best fulfill his function under the direction of a skilled public relations executive. He, in turn, should serve as a buffer for the chief executive, protecting him from what is often a predilection to dabble in this esoteric and alluring field so far removed in its techniques from the humdrum job of managing a company.

Yet the time may, and often does come, when the executive himself must engage personally in the political process as it affects his company.

Despite considerable talents in other respects, not every lobbyist is competent to present the case for his company effectively to a key politician where issues are of more than a passing complexity. There are exceptions to this, of course, since many lawyers adorn the calling—but they remain exceptions, and in any case the management executive usually knows the problem as well as his own attorney—perhaps better—besides bringing certain plus factors to the visitation. Always prestige conscious, the officeholder is flattered by a visit from the boss, and is fully aware that any contribution which may come his way when he next runs for office must have first received top executive approval.

Lobbying, which basically amounts to presenting information on a company, association, group or, for that matter, any party interested in legislative or administrative decisions, is an entirely legitimate undertaking and frequently an aid to the proper functioning of the democratic process. Danger threatens, however, when lobbying gets out of hand—when it exercises improper influence, growing out of either close personal relationships of the lobbyist with an official or from political contributions. In such cases the public utility is potentially far more vulnerable than a corporation not regarded as quasi-public in nature.

Knowing this, many highly placed utility executives support lobbying at national, state, and local levels on the very defensible ground that they simply desire to express a point of view affecting the welfare of their companies. To this they are justly entitled.

Because of Watergate, and what appears to be public revulsion over political corruption, some twenty-two states have approved legislation curtailing lobbying activities and establishing stringent standards for political contact activities. Perhaps the most aggressive move to curtail lobbying occurred in California where, in June, 1974, the people by a 70 percent vote approved a measure which may seriously inhibit any business, labor group, or others from making their views known to officialdom. This strikes a heavy blow at utilities which, because of the highly complex nature of their semipublic business, must continuously educate elected and appointed officials in such abstruse subjects as rates of return, rate base, costs of money, regulatory lag, use per customer, safety factors, franchises, and perhaps a dozen more. This is a world of law, of engineering, of accounting, and other modern disciplines, sometimes far removed from the experience or understanding of the legislator or administrator.

Yet utilities must learn to live with the lawful restrictions placed on certain types of advocacy, and this may not prove to be too difficult. It must be admitted that it is not necessary to wine and dine legislators, and place private airplanes at their disposal, to elicit their understanding or sympathy for company problems—helpful, perhaps, but not necessary.

So different approaches must be devised. These will be developed from the application of basic public relations principles which rest upon the bedrock of good judgment and the avoidance of the slightest appearance of a tainted relationship implying special privilege.

Closely allied to the necessity for the utility to express its viewpoint to public officials—either elective or appointive—through lobbyists, is the need to make political contributions to a candidate or a cause. Most, if not all, public utilities have found it desirable to proffer such contributions and most, if not all, have been exceedingly circumspect about this activity. There is a general recognition of the fact that giving political contributions entails elements of risk akin to walking through a public relations mine field, where explosive controversy may erupt at any moment.

Even before Watergate, utilities, in the main, were fully aware of the restrictions of the Corrupt Practices Act covering contributions to federal officeholders, and managed to escape unscathed when several officers of other giant corporations acknowledged culpability, suffered a storm of national criticism and, in most cases, paid their fines.

Most utilities, in making political contributions at any governmental level, take the position that such financial assistance is tendered solely to allow the utility to express a point of view, to "tell its story" to an official who will sit across the desk from a utility spokesman and *listen*. This is an important consideration to any public utility because of the enduring complexity of utility problems—far more difficult for the layman to understand than those afflicting almost any other kind of American industry.

Time and time again utility executives—meeting at various seminars and conventions—have stressed their hope to have politicians *listen* to their business troubles, as contrasted to the desire to *influence* political decisions.

In order to open political doors for the *listening* process—at the national level—many utilities have organized "good government clubs" of one kind or another among their top employees. These "clubs" solicit "voluntary" contributions from executives which are then placed in a political fund, usually administered by a committee appointed by utility management. It is this committee which selects the candidates and issues to be favored by contributions. A review of the recipients of contributions from utilities indicates that such candidates are of a conservative bent, and the issues receiving financial consideration are likewise conservative. The word "conservative" may be broadly defined, since utilities frequently assist forward-looking and progressive candidates, but tend to shrink—quite properly—from supporting those regarded as left wing or radical. The same may be said for issues. Certainly, no one could justifiably expect a utility executive to support financially a candidate or an issue pointing toward the destruction of his company, together with his source of livelihood.

Where the law permits local candidates and issues to accept political contributions from a corporation, many utilities brave public opinion by contributing in their own corporate names. These are usually listed in the press when the recipient complies with the law by filing his list of those who have financed his campaign.

There is some ultimate danger in this for the utility, of course, for with rising costs and higher rates for utility services the specter of a possible public ownership drive always lurks in the political background, and one of the early attacks on a utility might well focus on the political contributions it has made. Obviously, this is a factor which should be carefully considered by any utility and, in most cases, probably is before the contribution is made. With regard to the steps the utility takes in the political world, the advice of a skilled public relations practitioner, either on staff, or as a consultant, can be eminently helpful in order to avoid pitfalls.

The Utility
and
Its Publics

12

The Company You Love—Or Hate

THE OPERATIVE word in every utility's relationships with its public is *service*.

It is the be-all and end-all of company status in its communities. With prompt, dependable, and courteous service a utility may mount and prosecute an effective program of public relations. Without this priceless ingredient, such a program lacks force and persuasiveness.

Both experience and opinion surveys have demonstrated that other deficiencies may either be overlooked or forgiven by the customer, provided service is satisfactory. Using the same criteria, undependable and discourteous service tends to negate costly and professionally competent programs.

Compensatory rates are difficult to obtain where bad service prevails because in such instances the consuming public turns a deaf ear, organizes protesting groups, and frightens the commissioners of regulatory bodies. This results in the issuance of parsimonious decisions, which speeds the ever-worsening spiral of low earnings, deteriorating service, even lower earnings, and so on until, somehow, corrective measures are taken by management that reverse this trend.

Public relations executives, aware of the need for good service as an underpinning for their community relations programs, frequently run afoul of cost-conscious customer service managers who chip away at customer service in the belief that such downgrading will enhance earnings. Initially it does, enticing many top executives to succumb to the siren call, unaware that the penalty of such seduction is severe. The least disadvantageous result is either open or covert customer dislike, leading sometimes to the utility becoming the butt of public jokes by stand-up comedians, while the most disadvantageous is the threat of public ownership, egged on by ambitious politicians sensing the public's mood. Somewhere in between these extremes of attitude lies the image of a company out of step with its publics, one whose name instantly evokes an unfavorable picture in the public mind.

The first effort in the planned community relations program is an opinion survey, for without the results of such a sounding of public thinking there can be no competent program. From such a survey, consisting not only of a polling of opinion but also of depth interviews, the dimensions of the corporate image can be determined and the company's profile of its relationships with its publics may be drafted.

One of the necessities in developing a corporate image is the creation of a company creed which will endeavor to express in clear, concise language what the company stands for in its communities as well as the public interest principles which animate the company's corporate behavior.

Some company creeds contain explicit detail and, with what might be characterized as a boring verbosity, delineate the firm's public posture; but those creeds which seem to have greater public impact tend to be attention grabbers because of their sharp language and their brevity. As an example, one widely known utility with an award winning public relations program has published the following creed, and given it wide publicity in company offices, tour booklets, advertising, employee publications, films, and other media.

WE PLEDGE

To serve the [product] consuming public at the lowest possible rates and with a high standard of service; To conduct our business with courtesy and efficiency; To treat our customers

*honestly and fairly as we would like to be
treated; To deal frankly with those with whom
we do business at all times, and to be a good
citizen of the area we serve.*

The company creed may be regarded as a "copy platform," in the jargon of advertising executives or, if not a copy platform, at least a statement of company principle, to which the company proposes to adhere.

But after the creed, what?

The projection of company image itself is a complex undertaking which calls for the skillful and effective use of various kinds of communication media. Volumes could be—and have been—written on how to go about this most essential of public relations tasks. One of the best and most specific is, *Developing the Corporate Image*, edited by Lee H. Bristol, Jr., and drafted by thirty specialists, who furnished chapters in four fields: "Preparing to Meet the Problem," "The Faces of the Image," "Tools, Techniques and Media," and, "Where Do We Go From Here?"[4]

Within the past two decades, communications for public relations purposes have leaned heavily for content upon the work performed by the social scientists. One of the first to till this field was Rex F. Harlow, whose *Social Science in Public Relations* was a landmark in suggesting to public relations practitioners how people en masse might be motivated through an understanding of research into what prompts them to accept or reject a point of view.[5] Other volumes which might well be consulted by the executive interested in resting his messages upon scientific research are: *Human Behavior*, by Bernard Berelson and Gary A. Steiner,[6] and *Current Perspectives in Social Psychology*, edited by E.P. Hollander and Raymond G. Hunt.[7]

Until 1974 the development of a corporate image proceeded along what might be characterized as conventional lines. However, with ever-mounting inflation, the difficulty of obtaining capital at reasonable rates, and the general social unrest, new and imaginative programs were demanded from utilities' public relations planners. Accordingly, many companies are now engaged in reviewing their programs to bring them closer to today's requirements.

13

Winning Friends – and Influence

L IKE CAESAR'S wife or today's aspiring politicians, utilities and all business must remain above public suspicion, not easy in the prevailing opinion climate since Watergate.

Being credible becomes increasingly difficult with inflation requiring repetitious rate increases, the necessity to provide huge financial advances to assure energy supply, a need to construct plant against the opposition of ecologists, and provisions for higher costs all along the line.

Ultimately there is only one source of money, the customer, either industrial or domestic, who himself is wrestling with the conundrum of how to cope with his own increased costs—and finding no facile answers.

In past years a measure of solace for the beleaguered utility has rested in the public's acceptance of the regulatory process as providing a bulwark against a suspicion of corporate rapacity, but this confidence in governmental probity has long since disappeared. Today, steps which the utility finds it necessary to take in the interest of preserving service have led to a rising clamor from those who pay the monthly bills. In this opposition there exists a surprising element of bitterness, in contrast to the less virulent acceptance of the rising costs of gasoline, food, clothing, shelter, and other ordinary living expenses. These latter increases, although not accepted with total equanimity, rarely provoke more than a few forays by housewives into picketing lines at the supermarket, or a flurry of protesting letters to one's congressman.

On the other hand, let gas, electric, telephone, or water rates increase a few cents per month and the regulatory agencies are bombarded with angry letters and telegrams, and confronted with organized resistance that is translated into opposition appearances at public hearings. Newspapers, television, and radio reporters are quick to provide these protesters full and inflammatory publicity exposure.

During periods such as the present, when there is a desperate need to win and retain public confidence, the utility must draw upon whatever credit it has as a trusted corporate citizen of its service areas, much as a depositor draws upon his money in the bank, provided, of course, the utility through its past actions merits commendation or, at the worst, a grudging tolerance.

Many utilities have devised ways to establish credibility. Others are following belatedly, and a very few operate in the Neanderthal land of public dislike, dormant or active, which is apt in the one case to surface, or in the other to intensify, during periods when the utility's operations seem to run counter to the public's views.

Stratagems designed to elicit approbation are legion, limited only by the dearth of creative ideas, creative yet practical, for practicality is the *sine qua non* of successful public relations measures.

The sound basis upon which to seek public goodwill lies in the corporate *desire* to establish a friendly relationship with people in the mass—the adoption by executives and employees of mental attitudes which have no taint of superiority or arrogance, and are far removed from the idea that the public is essentially stupid, and therefore can be gulled. Attachment to the latter view is self-defeating and often self-destructive.

The desire to express goodwill and to expect the same from the public must permeate the complete utility establishment, from the board chairman to the president, on through the upper and middle management ranks, to the lowliest employee. Sincerity is truly the name of this game.

Involvement by company representatives in every reputable

civic and political group and in service clubs constitutes practical methodology. Such groups include chambers of commerce, youth organizations such as Boy Scouts and Camp Fire Girls, the United Crusade, charities formed to curb or cure a multitude of maladies such as The Heart Association, Multiple Sclerosis, the March of Dimes, American Cancer Society, Muscular Dystrophy, and on and on. Likewise, there are the organizations designed to aid the blind, the needy, the minorities, the scores of others which have proliferated since World War II. All should have on their boards of directors, or among their active supporters, employees of utilities—should have and often do. In pursuing such activities and assuming leadership positions in them—simply and easily accomplished because unpaid volunteers for charity are hard to come by—these utility employees create what has been defined as a good image for their companies. It is the expectation of those who contribute time in this manner that, aside from the value of community service performed, when it becomes necessary to increase rates, to build a new and controversial plant, or take some other unpopular step, the confidence they have won by their good works and the influence they have acquired will help to mute or soften protests. At the very least, they have become known and respected members of the community.

Communities are almost always led by opinion molders, those key individuals who by position, wealth, birth, achievement, or combinations of these attributes have achieved the enviable distinction of being quoted in the press when Establishment matters require comment. They are community leaders, they function as an elite corps in every large American city, and with remarkable unanimity. Every professional political campaign director has a list of their names on file in his office to be utilized instantly when the time comes to form a citizen's committee for one or another issue. Through their participation in community activities utilities must strive to become associated with those leadership groups which wield power in the political and public opinion fields. Politicians listen, because from the Establishment comes generous campaign contributions at election time, and people listen because spokesmen of the Establishment, mainly through media recognition, have become exemplars of the contemporary mythos.

Aside from the avenues of goodwill offered by community

groups, there remains another which is equally effective. This is the public school system.

Assemblies of students, as well as specialized classes, provide opportunities for furnishing information on the problems of energy, or for explaining the intricate story of the invention and progressive refinements of the telephone, for example. Some utilities regard school children as friendly ambassadors who foster their interests by carrying into their homes favorable impressions of the utility which, in turn, are transmitted to parents and perhaps other relatives.

This is why school domestic science groups and other science classes win the attention of utilities' school specialists who appear before them with various types of carefully designed instruction programs, all basically pointed toward accurately projecting a positive image of the company.

There are still other routes to community approbation, of course. One of the most necessary is that of contributing generously to worthy causes. Almost every utility is involved in tendering contributions, but in recent years there has been a slackening of this activity, mainly because regulatory bodies are beginning to insist that such largess be charged to the utility's stockholder-owners instead of being passed along to the customers who pay the monthly bills for service.

With passage of time and the multiplication of money-seeking groups, a few of the larger utilities have found it administratively desirable to shunt all charitable requests to a contributions supervisor for review. It is his task to winnow out the worthy applicants and reject the others by subjecting all of them to intensive, tough-minded scrutiny before passing any recommendations to upper management.

One expense which, without question, is borne by shareholders—or, in many cases by employees grouped in "good government clubs" (as previously mentioned)—is that which is classified as a political contribution. As government in its diverse ramifications has become more closely intertwined with business operations, such contributions have grown both in extent and amount. There is nothing intrinsically wrong with this practice, provided that it is conducted legally.

Worldly-wise utilities managers find it expedient to know the political office holders in their service areas, to study and categorize their philosophical leanings and, when campaign time rolls around, to support financially those who may be expected to consider utilities' problems in an evenhanded manner.

The record discloses that utilities have operated openly in this hazardous area, for in almost every instance the public filings of their political financial support have been duly published in the press and noted by eagle eyed reportorial commentators.

Such filings are, of course, now required by law, but even so, there may be a moral here: it may lie in the fact that public utilities, in contrast to many other businesses, are indoctrinated with the need to conduct their manifold operations in the light of day while curious and often critical regulators of one government level or another peer over their management shoulders.

Because of their hybrid characteristics, utilities have also become accustomed to inordinate interest of the media in their activities. Many have tried to satisfy this by making themselves always available to the press and the public but the ground rules are becoming increasingly difficult.

14

The Social Contract

IN THE SUMMER of 1975, the Watts section of Los Angeles, largely populated by blacks, had an unemployment rate for male blacks as high as 40 percent. Nationally, the unemployment rate for whites was about 8.5 percent. During 1964 seven Eastern cities had been stricken by black riots; and a year afterward Watts exploded. Some 144 hours later the final statistics were gathered, with 34 persons killed, 1,032 injured, 600 buildings damaged—200 of them totally destroyed by fire—and property loss estimated at $40 million.

Subsequently, a Governor's Commission on the Los Angeles riots, comprised mainly of Establishment members, held sixty-four meetings, took voluminous testimony, recognized unemployment as the "most serious immediate problem" facing the blacks as well as others of the poor and concluded:

> . . .there is an urgency in solving the problems, old and new, and. . . all Americans, whatever their color must become aware of this urgency. As we have said earlier. . ., there is no immediate remedy for the problems of the Negro and other disadvantaged in our community. The problems are deep, and the remedies are costly and will take time.

How deep and how costly the nation's utilities understand too well, for many have been in the forefront of those American enterprises contriving positive ways to shoulder their social responsibilities. Not that they have been too successful to date, because progress to overcome social inequities may not be measured in years, but only in decades, perhaps even in generations.

Nevertheless, the theory of social responsibility, as practiced by business generally, is now sufficiently consequential to prompt the American Management Association to formulate and offer an intensive three-day course in what it is; and what it is, as viewed by the AMA in its briefing outline, involves a series of questions. For example, should the corporation be responsible to: general public, stockholders, youth, minority groups, government, employees, others? Only Mortimer Snerd might be expected to answer, "No," to these queries contained in the bulletin of the AMA, which, among other ancillary subjects, lists "the law and corporate responsibility, profits and corporate responsibility, how to organize a corporate responsibility function," and more. For the public relations worker in a utility, the corporation has responsibilities in every conceivable area: to the general public, of course, in providing good service at the lowest possible rates consistent with a fair earning; to stockholders, who are entitled to that fair earning on their investment in the utility's properties; to employees, who require proper working conditions and prevailing wages; to government, which oversees integrity of operation; to youths, but most of all to the disadvantaged—not only blacks, Mexican-Americans, Puerto Ricans, but sometimes the whites, and sometimes women, all of whom may at any time show signs of militancy in their demands.

As long ago as 1967 the Equal Employment Opportunity Commission zeroed in on the problem of minority hiring. It reported that employment in utilities numbered 565,053, of whom 22, 042 were blacks, or 3.9 percent. Of the utilities' *white collar* work force at that time, only 1.7 percent were blacks. These discouraging figures led the EEOC to summon utilities executives to Washington, D.C., for a conference on minority hiring practices and to announce that staff representatives of the Commission would soon visit individual companies to review their minority hiring practices.

Complaints were heard not only on behalf of blacks. In 1963 the American Jewish Committee singled out public utilities—along with banking and transportation—as industries which discriminated against the "Jews and other minority groups."

On October 28, 1974, the Committee's top policymaking group, the National Executive Council, holding its semiannual meeting in Los Angeles, repeated its charge. It said consultations with the American Telephone & Telegraph Company were under way to seek more management positions there for Jews. Robert D. Lilley, A.T. & T. president in New York, added that his company and its affiliates "want to be certain that Jewish men and women are aware of any employment opportunities that we have. I'm certain. . . we will be able to increase the number of Jewish candidates interviewed and hired in management jobs."

When other utilities reviewed the charges made by the Jewish Committee, it became clear that all minorities cannot be considered for employment in the same frame of reference. For example, it developed that more Jews do not occupy executive offices in utilities mainly because of the inherently slow upward mobility in such management structures. This had inhibited company efforts to hire Jews.

This factor naturally does not apply to blacks or Mexican-Americans, and it certainly does not apply to women. Some blacks are handicapped by other drawbacks such as lack of education and skills, while many Mexican-Americans and other minorities must usually contend with the difficulties of expressing themselves in a second and foreign language.

All of these handicaps are being overcome by American utilities, in some instances by lowering employment standards to levels surmountable by the less skilled, and in other cases by lending employees as volunteers in depressed areas to give courses in simple English for foreign-born students.

The utilities have taken note of a comment by Roy Wilkins, of the National Association for the Advancement of Colored People:

No mere slogan can solve the complex racial and urban problems of our nation. Nor is there any single approach which, by itself, will bring total freedom to all Americans. The struggle cuts across almost every form of daily activity; it must be waged on every battlefield, including jobs, education, housing, voting and the law. Nor is this struggle confined to the deep South – it is nation-wide, and permeates the cities, the suburbs and the most remote rural areas.

It is one of the more pressing tasks of the public relations department of the utility to keep in mind the quasi-public nature of the company, which imposes a responsibility upon management only slightly less than that resting upon government agencies. This means that if any vestige of bigotry exists—and there have been charges that utility board rooms once exhibited WASP syndrome tendencies—it should be challenged and opposed as being contrary to both the company and the public interest.

By and large, however, utilities, as well as other segments of industry, and government itself, have contended with Sisyphean difficulties in minority job programs. Although in the field of communications—newspapers, radio, and television, and in motion pictures—minority employees have been highly visible in recent years, and although government has opened wide its doors to the underprivileged, there have been delays and setbacks which tend to validate the judgment of the Governor's Commission.

Typical of several efforts has been that mounted by Oakland, California, hailed as a "revolutionary" plan to provide 2,500 jobs with a $23 million grant from the Federal Economic Development Administration. The program was launched in the afterglow of the Watts riot. In three years only twenty new jobs materialized because, according to a report, "the program bogged down in a bureaucratic fight over minority hiring." The executive director of Oakland's antipoverty agency commented: "It's a pretty big disaster. A lot of commitments were made, but it never got off the drawing board."

Utilities have done better than this and so has private enterprise generally. While no statistics are immediately available, the utilities have come a long way since 1967. They saw the future clearly and while aspects may have been painful—requiring the lowering of standards, and the allocation of time, money, and personnel to educational efforts—they have recorded a notable success by observing established public relations principles. They have "identified the policies and behavior of an individual or an organization with the public interest and executed a program of action to earn public understanding and acceptance."

Consider the action of the Pacific Gas & Electric Company,

one of the world's largest investor-owned private utilities. As long ago as 1965, when students and other civil rights workers were battling the police at Selma, Alabama, the company provided two of its lawyers to go to the aid of those confronting Southern prejudice. A small action, but indicative of an important state of mind at that early date.

The decade since has been one of slow but considerable progress for the industry, as a walk into any utility branch office or attendance at any employee assembly will bear witness. The color of the faces, the contour of the eyes, tell the story.

15

Woodsman, Spare That Tree!

A YEAR before he died in October, 1975, renowned British historian Arnold Toynbee forecast that the world's developed countries would shortly be living in a "siege economy."

In an interview on his eighty-fifth birthday he said, "Man's plundering of nature now threatens him with pollution and depletion." He added that "few of the politicians of the developed countries have yet dared to tell the truth."

Maybe he overstated the case somewhat to sustain his imposing reputation as the prophet of doom and gloom, an accolade conferred when he sourly expressed the view that all civilizations eventually decay because they fail to respond to the challenges facing them.

But if he failed to score a bull's-eye, he was certainly circling the target, for in the late sixties the words "ecology" and "environment" struck the private sector with the cataclysmic force of a hurricane, and American utilities, like almost every other industry, were caught totally unprepared.

Hitherto, the world, with its oceans, its mountains, its forests, deserts, and plains, and what lay in or beneath, had been taken for granted by almost everyone. They were simply there, and they were there to be used, in keeping with ingrained historical precept. From the time the Mayflower landed, and the colonists felled their trees for their log cabins, shot their deer and wild turkeys for food, the pattern of despoliation grew and flourished. It was a pattern followed by the settlers drifting westward through the Cumberland Gap, by the mountain men plundering the virgin lakes and streams for beaver, by the buffalo hide hunters who slaughtered and left the meat to rot on the prairies, by the hydraulic miners who made heaps of rubble out of mountain meadows.

There was no other way. Men have conquered interplanetary space but man came into the world naked, his survival dependent upon what he could wrest from his habitation—animal skins for clothing, and the flesh of animals for food until a crooked stick taught him to cultivate the soil. From the very beginning, there has only been the earth and its unbelievably bountiful gifts for man—until now.

So man took, often prodigally, until one day someone thought to look into nature's cupboard and found it almost bare. Then the words "ecology" and "environment" took on new and poignant meaning.

American progress, with its high technology, was achieved only through the desecration of a continent. There was no other way, but the change from plenitude to scarcity, which seemed to come suddenly, was shocking in its implications, and brought a new word—depletion—into the current evaluation of our natural resources.

For the first time, we found we might not have enough to feed machines to say nothing of feeding people. In 1975 the Japan Fisheries Association publicly expressed the concern of 110 million people crowded into a land area less than that of California (with only twenty million) and with less than one-seventh of Japanese land arable. In a flurry of newspaper advertising in the American press, the Association inquired plaintively: "What will we all do?" Continuing: "Four billion. Seven billion." Then: "The first . . . represents the present world population; the second, the estimated population at the beginning of the next century . . . the population is mushrooming so fast we simply cannot produce enough food to keep pace with it." The advertising was not without a clearly expressed self-interest, since the association pointed out that Japan "must exert its best efforts toward making maximum use of its sea resources," in translation meaning Japan wants to fish where and however much it wishes, despite the tendency of others to establish 200-mile limits. From beyond the grave, old Thomas R. Malthus must be chuckling: "Two hundred years ago I told them, but they wouldn't listen."

Prospective lack of food was matched by far more immediate needs.

On one day there was enough oil, enough gasoline, enough natural gas, electricity, and water, in fact, plenty of almost everything. On the next, there was hardly anything, and everyone was scrambling for supply.

The utilities' world was turned topsy-turvy. One day they spent millions on advertising to woo customers and increase load; the next, in what must be the strangest industrial reversal in history, they were probably spending even more urging their customers to skip the daily shower, turn down their thermostats, and stumble around in their darkened homes.

To some, it appeared that we had become paupers through our profligacy; that instead of fooling Mother Nature we had fooled ourselves by wasting our resources in striving for ever higher living standards. To others, given the American promise of a better life for all, we had simply done what comes naturally. Whatever the rationale, there was no dodging the crisis.

Bad as this was, and is, there was, and is, something that might be considered equally disturbing. Steps to alleviate need found rough going in the swift rise of movements to protect the environment, whose supporters pressed their case with an almost religious fervor. They pushed and—in many cases—succeeded in getting legislation passed of restrictive and sometimes even oppressive character. Their efforts spawned swarms of "ecologists" and consultants of every stripe. Specializing in the protection of flora and fauna, they were found to be particularly adept at producing what the contemporary business shorthand called EIR's, environmental impact reports. Thus, those with a knack for words and a bowing acquaintance with elementary scientific claptrap were sought for gainful employment in a new and heady profession.

The numbers of these, all striving for a piece of the action, became mind-boggling. In fact, amoeba-like they proliferated so rapidly that the publishers of "Who's Who" were prompted to publish an *Environmental Protection Directory*, selling for $44.50, and offered to prospects with a suitably descriptive circular.

"Broad in Scope," they promised, and continuing: "Today, literally thousands of government agencies and private groups are committed to the fight to protect the quality of our precious resources, and study the effects of environmental factors upon human life."[8]

What does "environmental protection" include? The publishers' definition:

> *Use of public and private land, quality of air and water, preservation of wilderness and scenic areas, chemical and radiological contamination, noise, geologic phenomena, urban and roadside aesthetics, management and protection of water, soil, mineral, energy, wildlife, plant, forest and rangeland resources, and many, many more.*" (Not to be caught napping, the publishers provide a companion volume: *Consumer Protection Directory*, also billed as "broad in scope."[9])

No one can reasonably quarrel with the objectives of environmental and/or consumer crusaders. They are the inheritors of an idea whose time had come, but like other similar and strident movements in American life—against liquor, sexual naivete, or repressive employers—the tendency has been to push the pendulum, not to the center, but to the far side of the social spectrum. Nothing in moderation, which may be the hallmark of American culture, has, at times, given us prohibition and gangsters, pornographic movies and overt homosexuality, and many labor unions more powerful than any employers in many industries.

So, to their dismay, American utilities soon discovered that while the noose of scarcity around their necks was tight, the attacks of environmental buffs and their minions drew it even tighter. This when demands for their life-sustaining products were growing, not lessening.

Here, then, was a public relations challenge of the first order, crucial in its import, for the problem rested not so much in *finding* supply, difficult enough in any case considering demand, but mainly in steps to reach out, drill for it, build for it, or deliver it via pipeline, ship, or rail. Compounding what had all the earmarks of a dilemma was the fact that most of the major new sources were far away from the ultimate consumer.

As a typical example, a veritable Golconda of energy lay hidden deep under Arctic wastes, ready to offset the extortionate blackmail of Arabian nations. Yet one roadblock after another impeded production and delivery of this American owned resource. There were questions which threatened to hold up production for years. Would a natural gas or oil pipeline across Alaska adversely affect the annual migration of caribou? What about the permafrost overlaying the tundra—would that suffer irreparable damage? What about tanker deliveries of liquefied natural gas to harbors in the lower forty-eight states where re-gasification would take place? Was this safe? Should not long and intensive studies of "environmental impact" be required from the utilities as well as the drafting of EIR's? Certainly not only a few, but numerous regulatory approvals would be necessary for fixing price, as well as to satisfy the several conservation minded commissions empowered to hold hearings and hand down "yea and nay" decisions on any project.

Battle lines formed, and alternatives were considered.

Distraught producers of electric power, paying ever higher prices for fuel oil, sweated profusely when they clearly foresaw that within a relatively few years there might be no oil at any price, and turned toward nuclear power, to find they confronted a *mano a mano* controversy.

Late in the year 1975, twenty states were reported mulling bans on nuclear power development, the source that Washington, D.C., planners were hoping would supply 25 to 30 percent of the nation's power needs by 1985, compared with 8 percent now.

In California, which in 1975 had three nuclear power plants in operation and looked forward to twenty-eight more in the next twenty years, the public's approval was tested at a June, 1976, election. The ballot measure, an initiative, was supported by several conservation groups such as the Sierra Club, Friends of the Earth, and Project Survival who were determined, they said, to force advocates of nuclear power to prove unmistakably and publicly that its use is safe.*

* By a vote of more than two to one—1,270,084 to 524,655, California voters on June 8, 1976, rejected the Nuclear Power Initiative, supported by environmentalists, and providing for stringent safety standards for new nuclear plants. The defeat was partially attributed to the action of the California State Legislature which, just a few days before the vote, approved a series of measures establishing safety standards for nuclear plants less severe than those incorporated in the ballot measure. After the battle, proponents claimed a partial victory, asserting their ballot proposal triggered the legislative enactment.

Crisis of Confidence

While opposition to nuclear power apparently hardened, it was worth noting that the Harris Poll, as of August 18, 1975, reported 63 percent of the American people accepted civilian nuclear energy as clean, inexpensive, and safe. Only 19 percent opposed construction of more such plants, while only 5 percent expressed fears with regard to safety.

On still another front, the desperate search for more oil to produce power was sidetracked, at least temporarily, by the public and legal resistance of many groups, some with acronyms on their banners, such as SOS (Save Our Shores) and GOO (Get Out Oil). Leasing of offshore Federal oil lands was laid on the table until the controversies might be adjudicated. This California opposition found support in the action of a coalition of forty Southern California cities and counties, somewhat gradiosely self named the Council of Local Governments Concerned with Federal Proposals for Oil Development on the Outer Continental Shelf, that voted to seek court action to halt leasing.

Fortunately for those seeking future oil and gas supply, and in no sense judging the claims of conservationists, approval to construct the Alaskan pipeline was finally pried from reluctant authorities who had anguished over the decision for years, wavering back and forth in the winds of legislative and bureaucratic indecision. Despite the pressures, they acted at long last, very, very late in terms of the frightening necessity, but ultimately yielding to the public educational campaign mounted by the utilities and the oil companies.

This public relations campaign, which has never ceased and is even now underway, presented difficulties in at least two respects.

First, it was hard to conceal a built-in element of self-serving, no matter how deftly the identification of need was shifted to the consumer. Second, Americans, conditioned over the years by intensive advertising where wants and consumption were artificially created, were simply emotionally and intellectually incapable of conceiving that a day might come when there would be no gas at the burner tip, no electric lights, no heat for a frosty morning. All such necessities and innumerable comforts, too, had always been available at their fingertips. How *could* there be change?

That was really the nub of the public relations problem—this question of believability. Without that matchless component the selling of any idea to the public becomes very difficult, indeed.

Gradually, but with glacial slowness, this skepticism, partially tinged by suspicion and distrust of both business and government leadership, is being dissipated, but there is still a very long way to go and current opinion surveys are hardly encouraging. Executives of the public and private sector have taken to the stump to explain and to convince. They have talked from whatever rostrum is available and they have tried, with varying degrees of success, to simplify the complex. Advertising has carried the message, as well as pamphlets, and also as word-of-mouth, united to tell the story of lack and of need. With all the obstacles of construction, of government approvals, of public distrust, maybe there is still enough time—just maybe.

16

Truth– or Some Consequences

W HEN THE MEDIA demand answers, a public rela-tions department occasion-ally confronts alternatives.

There are four options: Tell the truth, all of it. Tell part of the truth, fudging a little, here and there. Lie. Or maintain silence.

In the long—and even the short—run, the best of these is to tell the truth, every mind-boggling, inexplicable, indefensible bit of it, no matter how badly it hurts. Admittedly there are times when it hurts very badly: for example, if you happen to be the CIA and have secretly spent millions to topple a foreign government, or the FBI wiretapping a celebrity's bedroom, or a President of the United States knee-deep in Watergate. These examples, while notorious, are not unique. As a matter of fact, it took Washington, D.C., author David Wise a book of 600 pages suitably to chronicle the lying, deception, and secrecy of government.

Private industry, and particularly its public utilities sector, can hardly hope ever to compete with the record so meticulously compiled by Mr. Wise.

In fairness, though, it should be acknowledged that whatever the propensity of the business executive toward probity, it is not necessarily congenital like a birthmark; far more often it is some-thing acquired over the years, like a taste for anchovies. Decades ago, most businessmen, and all utility executives with the brand of

Insull burned into their memories, found that lying publicly is self-defeating in view of the heavy odds on being caught at it and the horrendous penalties that seem to follow inescapably.

This did not come as news to public relations professionals, aware that it is only pragmatic to practice honesty as a most rewarding policy, apart from moral implications, and in the teeth of prospective suffering contingent on being trapped *in flagrante delicto*.

Truth telling is therefore held to be synonymous with establishment of credibility, which equates with being able to stay alive in the shark infested world of public opinion. This concept they have taken pains to impress upon utilities bosses, pointing out how benefits accrue from an addiction to veracity. In the main, they prevailed, for you may search the record and find few, if any, instances of outright lying by leaders of the utility industry.

With overt deception eliminated as a refuge, what other tactic remains to evade a probing inquisition?

Two other havens offer shelters of a sort. Both have been sought upon occasion, but neither promises a restful night's sleep for that public relations officer required to field questions dangerous to the company's well-being.

One recourse is to tender a judicious mixture of the truth with fantasy, but this type of response must be considered only a temporary ploy these days when check and countercheck by media sleuths uncover contradictory leaks in the most unexpected places.

There remains, finally, the stubborn retreat into silence, signified by the tight-lipped, "No Comment," which theoretically blocks further inquiry. Corporate spokesmen may seek this sanctuary when unwilling to confess delinquencies. It also happens to be the storm cellar for the malefactor fleeing the torment of a grand jury or a Congressional committee after "taking the Fifth."

Still, hunkering down in the winds of adverse public opinion and saying absolutely nothing may, at times, prove preferable to talking. It just may be the better choice between two evils, with the selection determined by the exercise of public relations judgment. Should the decision be to lie doggo, and resist pressures to speak, it is difficult to escape an inference of guilt. On occasion it is deemed expedient to soften the "no comment" strategy to the phrase "neither confirm nor deny," but this subterfuge is also fraught with the same infirmity.

Only two decades ago some service industries such as railroads and public utilities considered it unwise to provide certain facts for the media. Railroads were inclined to preserve silence about wrecks and casualties until their own personnel could assess damage. Utilities were likely initially to profess ignorance of the details when structures were destroyed by a natural gas explosion or leveled by fire starting from faulty electric wiring or destruction and deaths followed a broken dam.

Stalling for time thus became a standardized technique in the mistaken hope that delay might lead to formulation of a more palatable story than the facts actually warranted. Corollary to this was the realization that news marches on and that what may rate as a page one sensation today may prove a bore tomorrow when other news, possibly even more sensational, competes for the headlines and reader attention.

But, like news, time marches on. Opinion surveys and studies in the behavioral sciences, plus ever-growing sophistication in the informational arts, have brought a sharp reversal in communication procedures.

Only in the most backward railroad or public utility might one today find a tendency to withhold or suppress news of a disaster. The contrary is the rule. Responsible public relations executives now develop—sometimes really dig—facts from often reluctant operating supervisors and proffer the results to the media, even though those facts may brew a bitter tea.

There may be times when a situation of extreme corporate delicacy counsels prudence with publicity. For example, if a utility is engaged in perfectly legal competitive undertakings or market strategies which could be wrecked by untimely disclosure, there is no compulsion in the current ethos of utilities responsibility to tell all—or anything. The test of withholding disclosure is whether either the public trust or the public interest is likely to be violated. If not, the activity in question may be considered privileged, its immunity to publicity justified, similar to cases when the government invokes the excuse of "national security" for its shield.

These kinds of company security issues are rare. In almost every instance, the public relations practitioner should opt for full disclosure.

17

Untilled Fields

THE COMMUNICATIONS skills exhibited by utilities in dealing with their publics on critical issues somehow do not extend to their retired employees or their shareholders. Here they rate an "A" for apathy, not an "E" for excellence.

Consider the employee who for nearly forty years worked for the Company, and the fact of his working for the Company had become in itself a mark of status in his own mind, and a prestige symbol in the minds of others. Then the day came when they gave him a watch, or a tape recorder, or golf clubs (the cost of the gift depending on his rank), praised him for his fidelity, and said goodbye. For him the party was both sad and joyous; sad because a long, intimate relationship had ended, but happy, too, in a way, because now he could enjoy a long, leisurely breakfast and afterward have the whole day to himself, to do exactly what he wanted.

All at once— and it seemed all at once, although he had counted the days and minutes—he was free of responsibility, the umbilical cord of work severed, his time his own. Not until the checks began to come from the Company, and from social security, did it really dawn on him that he had been turned out to pasture, just like a horse. He would pull no more wagons, run to no more fires. In the delicate euphemism of the Company personnel department he had become an "annuitant" or a "retiree"—words devised to avoid the harsher but less evasive designation—"pensioner."

Whatever the term, the loyalty which was deeply rooted in those years of service to the Company remained as firm as ever. If the Company were in trouble, certainly he would like to help in any way he could. He wanted the Company to do well. He wanted to protect the Company. He was ready, even eager, to support it in all its manifold operations. He was, he felt, still a part of it.

Since his name was carried on the mailing list, he received a copy of The Magazine. This kept him currently advised of activities such as supply and equipment problems, financial needs, the appeals to regulatory bodies, technological advances, and the always interesting personnel changes and promotions, pending retirements—and deaths. All were stories of import to him and to the others who functioned in a little world of their own.

Sometimes they wondered why they were not asked to do something—such as supporting the Company's need for higher rates, or a new city franchise, or authority to purchase and bring additional energy from faraway places. They would willingly, even gladly, talk these up among their friends and neighbors, their fellow club and church members, their chance acquaintances—only, no one asked. Besides, they required direction and the "party line" which, although furnished by the Company to others in memoranda and "position papers," were never furnished to retirees. Therefore, in a public relations sense, they constituted an untilled field. Although many could help they were rarely used or, if so, then almost clumsily.

Another aspect existed regarding this tenuous relationship with *their* Company. They were aware, through reading the periodic magazine, that salary and wage increases were being granted with clocklike regularity every year to those still on the payroll. They were also painfully aware that nothing had been added to their own monthly pensions. The Company seemed to have acknowledged the pressures of inflation on their working employees, and had managed to win new and higher rates for its own products and services. But the retirees had built the Company, they told themselves. So they had another reason for alienation, but because of deep attachment for the Company they were not particularly bitter. They would still help if asked and given the party line on issues.

As for the shareholders, some were great and powerful institutions, others were personally affluent and unlikely to get concerned over tribulations of a corporation in which they had invested. The majority were ordinary folk who bought utilities stocks that had established impeccable records for dividend stability and seemed relatively unaffected by distortions in the economy.

Although shareholders comprise a receptive audience, prepared to explain and support a position, they are not often used effectively, if at all. Instead, their contacts with the Company of which they own a portion are usually limited to a glance at the quarterly earnings reports which come along with the dividend checks and to the annual reports. Orthodoxy prescribes that the latter, in particular, be drafted in a mixture of financial and legal prose having the effect of inducing slumber instead of enticing one to read. So the shareholder, like the annuitant, is frequently among the missing when the battle to sway public opinion is joined.

Such failure of many utilities' public relations departments to utilize efficiently the communication vehicles available is hard to explain and even harder to defend.

While closely reasoned and professionally adept communication programs are prosecuted on many fronts—in fact, among any and all groups willing to listen—the former employee and the stockholder have been accorded the sort of treatment characterized by Daniel P. Moynihan as "benign neglect."

If the working employee, as public relations textbooks are fond of pointing out, is the Company's first line of communication, then certainly the retired worker and the stockholder, equally strongly motivated, must be regarded as the second.

An instructive lesson underscoring this concept was furnished by the oil companies at the height of the oil embargo. Knowing they were targets of criticism for asserted failure to foresee and provide for gasoline shortages, their public relations departments flooded the mails with long, explanatory letters to their pensioners and their stockholders, exhorting them to action, and arming them with the methods of combating public attack.

Not only that, the oils, in contrast to the lackluster performances of some utilities at the beginning of the inflation surge, provided what they called "cost of living" bonuses as supplements to their pension payments. Hardly anything could be calculated to inspire a warmer, friendlier spirit than this employee relations gesture, resting, as it did, upon the timeworn adage that "money talks."

Such actions of the oils predictably brought the expected result. Hundreds of voluntary letters, extolling the integrity and farsightedness of the oils, began to grace the newspaper editorial pages of the nation, while many an impromptu speech, well larded with facts, was heard from the rostrums of service clubs, P.T.A. gatherings, and even during neighborly chats over backyard fences.

Private
VS.
Public Ownership

18

————

An Ounce of Prevention

"WHY," ask some utility customers, "should not the public own and operate companies that provide basic necessities such as natural gas, electric power, water, and the telephone?"

This question is not new. The idea that motivates it has lain dormant in segments of the public mind for decades. Once in a while it surfaces and takes on form and purpose, and when that happens the utility which may be affected must be prepared to answer.

Farsighted companies have adopted the public relations practice of planning on the possibility of being required to face the issue of public ownership, although it may appear only in discussions among friendly groups, where their employees are on the defense.

Thus, to be helpful to their employees, and at the same time be at least partly prepared to counter an organized attack should one be mounted, many utilities have developed what they term "hip pocket" information supporting the principle of investor-ownership of public utilities. They readily admit their views are subject to what might appear plausible rebuttal but point out that in the world of social and economic ideas there are few, if any, absolutes; that it is believing that makes it so.

Their arguments run as follows:

1. Every publicly owned utility reflects an erosion of the American system of private enterprise.

A. The proper function of a democratic, elected government is to govern. To own and operate businesses in competition with investor-owned companies is not a proper function of government. Such government intervention can only be condoned when private enterprise fails or is unwilling to provide service.

B. Governments should not operate on the principle of spending taxpayers' money on projects which obviously decrease potential tax income.

2. Utilities owned by government do not pay their way in supporting necessary governmental services.

A. So-called "in lieu" payments by municipally owned utilities to city treasuries are not equivalent to the taxes paid by investor-owned utilities of the same size or scope.

B. Homeowners and other taxpayers must assume more than a fair share of the tax burden because publicly-owned utilities are exempt from federal and state income taxes, local property, and franchise taxes.

C. Publicly owned utilities are funded by tax-exempt bond money, giving them an unfair advantage over investor-owned companies.

3. If utilities are municipally owned, why not extend the principle to oil, steel, aircraft, missile and spacecraft, airline, and other companies? In other words, why should the government not own almost everything?

A. History demonstrates that people benefit more in a private enterprise economy with profit incentives. Under the capitalistic system the American economy has provided more wealth for more people than any previous economy in history, despite admitted inequities which we are in process of overcoming.

4. Efficiency suffers, for the bureaucratic environment of a municipally owned utility does not lend itself to management ingenuity and effective employee performance. Experience of the individual with government at all levels supports this view.

5. Municipal utilities are not profit inspired and therefore lack the incentive to perform efficiently.

A. Example: A huge municipally-owned electric utility has one employee for every 127 customers. In adjoining territory an investor-owned competitive utility has one worker for every 215 customers. Could less costly and more efficient operating procedures be attributed to the compulsion provided by stockholders and regulatory agencies? Or because government workers are shielded from supervisory discipline through civil service tenure?

6. Takeovers of investor-owned utilities by government cost taxpayers sizable sums for purchase from their private owners, with doubtful benefit.

7. Safety, rates, and operations of private utilities are major considerations by management, if for no other reason than the strict regulation by agencies established by the public for that purpose. This is in contrast to the political supervision exercised by city councils or mayors, who lack the required expertise for such a responsibility. The carrot of cheap rates, used to entice voters, is usually illusory in view of the possible deterioration of service and tax evasion.

19

Pie in the Sky

NEARLY TWO decades ago, a study of public ownership in one segment of the utilities industry was undertaken by the writer. Titled "Public Ownership in the Gas Utility Field," it appeared in the *Public Utilities Fortnightly* of October 10, 1957. Its conclusions were clear: while it appeared that the *numbers* of municipal systems were increasing—doubling from the period 1950 to 1957—they still served comparatively few customers, and therefore could hardly be considered a threat to private ownership.

In that far-off and less turbulent period, the motivation for forming publicly-owned systems was one of simple economics, plus a need for service where investor-owned companies declined to extend costly lines into "thin" areas where inadequate sales would place a cost burden upon other customers. The public groups, inspired many times by the glowing reports of certain bond houses and engineering firms, found government financing at very low interest rates easy to come by.

The years intervening since those days have witnessed no upsurge in drives toward public ownership of any utilities, but on occasion there may occur an exception to this generalization. A case in point is that of Berkeley, California, where the city mounted an abortive effort to take over its electric service from an investor-owned company. The voters rejected the attempt.

Even so, the present is a time for exercising a wary vigilance. The nation is undergoing profound change, wherein many of its institutions are being scrutinized and, in some cases, challenged. Unemployment, shrinking incomes, rising costs, a suspicious and even hostile electorate, a resentment against business—all stir the muddy waters in which dissidents and their demagogic spokesmen find good fishing.

An experienced commentator once observed that a public ownership attack occurs when spark and powder come together; almost any combination of circumstances may trigger a move. To guard against being taken unaware it is necessary to lean upon intermittent surveys of public opinion, not only of the nose counting variety, but also those of the depth interview type. On the results of these will depend the public relations programs to be created.

But if the threat of a public ownership move becomes a reality, despite every effort and suitable precaution, what steps may be taken to save a property?

First and most important is the retention of an experienced, professional campaign management firm to supervise the company's defense and counterattack.

The campaign directors will be responsible for developing an overall plan, the theme, organizing citizens' committees to support the concept of private enterprise as contrasted to public ownership, and preparing a budget listing all proposed expenditures.

Such steps must be taken *before* the campaign battle actually gets underway.

In most instances, public groups, no matter how strong their ideological urge to put government into the utilities business, have experienced serious difficulties in raising money to finance their attack. As a matter of fact, the hard task of collecting an adequate war chest with which to pay for the many expenses to be incurred—a staff, advertising in newspapers, radio and television, office space, printing, research—has many times caused zealots to shelve plans for a public ownership campaign before they were well underway.

With the rise of consumerism, and the shift toward a heightening dependence upon government to solve all of our social and economic ills, it is prudent for utilities public relations executives to keep sharp eyes on public sentiment in their service territories.

As long ago as 1952 the late Donald D. Hoover, then president of a national public relations firm serving the electric power industry, was warning his clients of possible dangers. In the issue of November 20, 1952, of the *Public Utilities Fortnightly*, he cited a Gallup poll of 1937 showing that "among all voters of that time, public ownership was preferred two-to-one over private ownership of the electric industry." This happened to be a period of heavy unemployment, as the country fought to emerge from the depression of the early thirties. Later, between 1943 and 1951, as the economy turned upward, polls revealed a drop of about one-third in support for some sort of government ownership, Hoover said.

With the national economy again in a downtrend, consumers in November, 1974, picketed electric rate increase hearings of the California Public Utilities Commission with signs reading: "God said: 'Let there be light.' The utility says: 'If the price is right.' "

The consumer spokeswoman, representing a group named Toward Utility Rate Normalization (TURN), said: "I am here to tell this Commission that we consumers have had enough."

In January, 1975, display advertising appeared in California newspapers on the financial pages:
"Are you sick and tired of
Excessive Rate Increases
By the Profit Making
PUBLIC UTILITY SERVICE COMPANIES???
We are! We want to try to do
something about it. If you are
interested and want to help, send
a self-addressed STAMPED envelope to:
S.M.C. P.O. BOX 4132
Inglewood, Ca. 90304."

As consumers hardened their resistance to rate increases in the recent recession period, a survey by *Practical Public Relations*, a semimonthly newsletter published in Rochester, N.Y., points to significant cutbacks in public relations expenditures by major American corporations in 1975.

Of 2,460 corporate public relations directors responding to a questionnaire, 52 percent said that budgets for outside public relations services had been cut for 1975. Despite these cuts the survey reported a "gigantic" emphasis on governmental relations, and a growing emphasis on "consumer rights programs."

The report did not disclose how many public utilities responded, but there can be little doubt that public service companies are giving ever more attention to ways of meeting the growing threat of customer groups who, with their own pocketbooks squeezed by rising costs, are indifferent to the often desperate need of the regulated utility.

Both internal and external meetings of public relations executives might well be held to plan how to cope properly with problems, present and future, associated with public opinion trends.

Specialists in directing campaigns against public ownership could be called in to offer case histories of past attacks on utilities and how they have been won or lost.

These would be particularly illuminating. As an example, a decade ago a group was formed in a major American city with the avowed purpose of placing one of the nation's largest energy distributing companies under public ownership.

Heavy advertising was published in the press demanding a takeover, but the identities of the sponsors of the move were carefully hidden. A quick investigation by the utility with the aid of professional public relations personnel led to unmasking the prime movers of the ploy. The next step was a demand by the city council for an in-depth probe of the attack. The publicized drive for public ownership of the utility promptly collapsed. It has not been revived, and is mentioned simply to indicate how instructive it is to consider the case histories of such efforts.

Aside from the need to keep generally informed, the public relations practitioner is sobered by the reflection that continuation of the principle of private ownership of utilities always rests in the hands of voters who have ready access to the ballot box. So here we confront an element of social sufferance, where billions of dollars in properties might sometime be at hazard. One is moved to hope that the words of James Madison may not prove prophetic:

"Wherever the real power in a government lies, there is the danger of oppression. In our Government, the real power lies in the majority of the community."

In our Bicentennial era we might remember Thomas Jefferson who had a cautionary word for that majority:

"Agriculture, manufacture, commerce and navigation, the four pillars of prosperity, are the most thriving when left to individual enterprise."

Shadows in the Sun

THESE ARE perilous times for all business and particularly for the quasi-public corporation known as a utility. Only the most perceptive among utility managements and public relations experts seem to comprehend fully the character of the present epoch, which is one of dynamic change in every aspect of our lives.

Men schooled in the management techniques of business administration, finance, law, accounting, engineering, and even conventional economics, go to their desks each day, confront their regular workaday tasks, and perform their usual duties often in blissful ignorance of what should be their most crucial undertaking: saving the private ownership system in the United States.

Extravagant rhetoric? No, right on target, particularly if one considers all the elements of the case objectively, tossing overboard first of all some of our concepts to which we have become attached. The first to be jettisoned might well be the phrase, "free enterprise," part of the enduring folklore of capitalism, a shopworn holdover from the nineteenth century, a hackneyed shibboleth once specifically descriptive but long since divorced from economic reality.

For the question is, what enterprise is "free" if we accept the definitions of "having no trade restrictions," or "not subject to government regulation," or "not hampered or restricted" in "its normal operation," which Mr. Webster says are synonymous with "free?" In these terms hardly anyone is "free," and least of all the regulated public utilities.

Even so, something worse may be in the offing, if recent comments of businessmen, politicians, academicians, pollsters, and others are given credence.

Item: Appearing before the California Bankers Association in May, 1975, Jerome W. Hull, chairman of the Pacific Telephone & Telegraph Company, said that American enterprise is "in mortal peril," mainly because the United States educational system teaches children about "socialism, communism, and other such ideologies, but very little about capitalism." He blamed legislators and the media for the "public's economic ignorance," which he said encourages the people's "lack of confidence in, and distrust of, business and industry." He added that polls show the public has lost much of its confidence in "medicine, religion, business, and banks," and recommended we "should be talking about our heritage with great pride," citing the long list of economic and social advances made over the last two centuries.

Item: Chairman Thomas A. Murphy of General Motors, meeting at the annual stockholders' session in June, 1975, said newspaper editorials, political speeches, and opinion surveys frequently "demonstrate a growing distrust, if not hostility, toward business." Continuing, "They foster suspicion that our economic system itself, free enterprise (sic), call it what you will, no longer is adequate for our times." He added: "We ask no favors. We ask only freedom from unreasonable regulation."

Item: The Gallup poll announced in May, 1975, that on American college campuses a strong anti-business mood prevails and there is a widespread lack of knowledge of the American economic system. The same survey disclosed that only 20 percent of the students believes that the moral and ethical standards of business executives are high or very high. In contrast, college teachers were given a rating of 70 percent—the highest of the 11 occupations listed. Political officeholders ranked next to lowest, 9 percent, and advertising practitioners lowest, 6 percent.

By a margin of nearly two-to-one, students believe the government should place stricter controls on business, and by a percentage of 54 percent to 39 percent favor breaking up big companies into smaller companies. *By a vote of 87 percent to 11 percent, students* agree that people in business are concerned too much with profits and not enough with public responsibility. They also favor stricter government controls on labor.

The survey further showed that college students are twice as likely to consider themselves to the left of a liberal-conservative scale as they are to the right—in itself the foreboding of an ominous future.

Item: M.A. Wright, chairman and chief executive officer of Exxon, U.S.A., in a speech at the annual Business Conference at Rutgers University, June, 1974, said that all companies are in danger of government takeover. Meanwhile, Gilbert F. Richards, president and chief executive officer of the Budd Company, observed in an interview: "People today don't trust government—or business, or labor. All three of us better make sure they get it back and we better do it together."

Item: Opinion Research Corporation reported in 1971 that a survey revealed 87 percent of those polled indicated "little or moderate" approval of business, the "little approval" having risen from 47 percent in 1965 to 60 percent in 1971, and "high approval" dropping from 20 percent in 1965 to 11 percent in 1971. In August, 1975, pollsters reported another change—for the worse. Hart Research Associates, in a poll for the leftist People's Bicentennial Commission, announced that their survey indicates one-third of the American people believe the capitalist system is past its peak; 49 per cent believe big business is the source of much of what is wrong with the economy; 56 percent would "probably support" or "definitely support" a presidential candidate who favored "employee ownership or control of business."

Troubled by the general malaise affecting the private sector, *Time* magazine, on February 14, 1972, published its concern:

Free enterprise should be valued, preserved, and strengthened. . . Only in the United States are airlines, radio and television networks, telephone systems, and all other major industries owned primarily by private individuals. . .Recently, however, free enterprise in the United States has been under heavy pressure. . .Does free enterprise have much of a future? If so, what should be done to preserve and strengthen the system? If not, what will replace it?

For some, the answer to this almost plaintive query regarding the future of the system seems somehow to contain in itself a premonitory implication that the patient is already on his death-bed.

Will and Ariel Durant, having published their monumental ten-volume, *The Story of Civilization*, followed with a synthesis, *Lessons of History*, including a chapter on "Socialism and History":

> *Year by year the role of Western governments in the economy rises, the share of the private sector declines. . .The fear of capitalism has compelled socialism to widen freedom, and the fear of socialism has compelled capitalsism to increase equality.* East is West, and West is East, and soon the twain will meet. (Emphasis supplied.)[10]

The historians' concept is echoed by economists—or at least some of them.

As an example, J.K. Galbraith, in his volume, *"The New Industrial State,"* wrote:

> *Increasingly, it will be recognized that the mature corporation, as it develops, becomes part of the larger administration complex associated with the state. In time the line between the two will disappear. Men will look back in amusement at the pretense that once caused people to refer to General Dynamics and North American Aviation and AT&T as* private business.(Emphasis in original.)[11]

The Accidental Century, by Michael Harrington, develops the theme that capitalism is dying, to be replaced by a socialist society. His opening sentence:

> *In the Twentieth Century, something enormous is being born, and something enormous is dying. This book is about what is dying. It is about the contemporary decadence.* And from his final chapter: *Either Western man is going to choose a new society or a society will choose, and abolish him. . .America has for some time been engaged in the wrong argument. It has been debating as to whether the future should be collective and social and ignoring the fact that the present is already becoming so. The real issue is not whether, but how, this future will arrive–unwittingly or consciously chosen.*[12]

Daniel Moynihan, recently elected U.S. Senator from New York, spoke before a national association of advertisers in 1972. He

discussed what he termed the "business ethics of late capitalism."
He said:

> It seems to me that late capitalism, with these conditions, is charac-
> terized by a precipitous decline in the legitimacy of business in-
> stitutions and governing institutions generally and the onset of a
> post-industrial, post-capitalist society. (Emphasis supplied.)

Page Smith, prizewinning author and historian, writing in
the *Los Angeles Times* on May 29, 1974, said he believes

> . . . that the United States is much closer to a genuinely revolu-
> tionary situation than one might guess.

So here we have over the short span of a few years a sampling
of reputable voices from the business world, the media, the
pollsters, the campuses and the halls of ivy, all expressing concern
or heralding change, and we witness the creation of Amtrak and the
new postal service, the government rescues of Lock-
heed and Penn Central, and other significant departures from
laissez-faire.

Certainly, this is a world and an economic system apart,
totally foreign to that of William McKinley, Calvin Coolidge, Herbert Hoover or that even of Dwight D. Eisenhower. Nor could
those gentlemen understand a nation which supports millions in
idleness from the cradle to the grave, provides health services for
the indigent without cost, dispenses help in the form of unso-
licited checks from the national treasury to the country's elderly and
sustains the unemployed with regular payments over a continuously extended period. Along with these massive redistributions of
wealth—the taking from those who have, and the giving to those
who have not and could not possibly get otherwise—there are
countless other ways of altering society that have been devised under
the cruel lash of national necessity. Among these are the funding of
jobs for minorities, slum clearance programs, transit plans, and
even such educational projects as basket weaving and square danc-
ing.

Faced with what Grover Cleveland might characterize as a
condition, and not a theory propounded by those who have gazed
at tea leaves and seen the outline of a darkling future, what are the
public relations imperatives for the public utility in this era of
change?

There are two: become so strongly identified with the public interest in the minds of the communities served that antagonists will be hesitant to attack; if attacked and threatened with public takeover, mount a professional, effective campaign.

21

Total Commitment

GIVEN the ever-increasing public hostility and distrust of business, together with the inherent dangers implicit in the rising price structure caused by the inflationary push, it is doubtful that private enterprise including the utility can turn back the historical clock.

The victory lies in keeping things as they are; not in the sense of resisting inevitable and worthwhile change but in defending the institutions and systems in which we believe.

This is the objective to which the utility must address itself with far greater intensity than at present. This is the central theme about which all of its public relations activities should ultimately revolve.

Why is the public utility singled out for what appears to be its historic task? Because in our economic and governmental structure the public utility represents our finest example of being neither fish nor fowl. It is partly public, and partly private, a notable instance of a strikingly efficient enterprise dedicated to serving all the people under strict government regulation. Because of its special and unique character it is most vulnerable to attack and takeover by government ownership advocates who contend the public should own and manage enterprises that provide natural gas, electricity, water, communications, and transportation.

In the case of transportation, the record of bureaucrats and politicians has proved a sorry mess. In certain urban areas they have snarled proposed solutions for city transportation in bureaucratic red tape and continuous "surveys" which cost taxpayers untold millions, with no end in sight. A prime example is that of a politician elected mayor of one of the nation's largest cities with the pledge that he would "shovel earth" for a mass transit system within eighteen months. It is now about three years since and the city has been engaged in another survey, this one costing $300,000.

Hitherto, public utilities, immersed in the public opinion problems attendant on obtaining compensatory rates to avoid drowning in red ink, have been preoccupied with building their community images along orthodox public relations lines. This is both necessary and commendable, and to the prosecution of the objective of creating image, the better programs have devoted a total communications effort, always a requisite for success.

Now the times call for a complete reassessment of these programs by utility chief executives and the managers of their public relations efforts.

There are only two choices: continue along the present public relations course which, considering the opinion climate, risks a takeover by government within a relatively brief period measured by history's clock, or *finally face the issue boldly with a total commitment of communications resources to supporting the concept of private ownership of utilities.*

To those utility executives who are aware of the immensity of the stakes involved but who have until now shrunk from the necessity of overt confrontation, there still remains the gut fear of rousing sleeping dogs and the fervent hope that if you don't talk about it, maybe it will go away.

Evidently "it"—the move toward nationalization—will not go away, if we credit the reliability of our senses. Italy, Portugal, and France move leftward, while even Great Britain, once, with the United States, the great defender of economic private enterprise, now totters on the brink, too late for rescue. On October 30, 1974, headlines in the *Los Angeles Times* told the story: "Wilson's Socialist Program Outlined by Queen," and in the *Los Angeles Herald-Examiner*: "Queen Elizabeth Announces Major Economic Reforms." From the *Times* account:

> . . . *the words of the Queen recited Tuesday [in the House of Lords]*

would have warmed the heart of any revolutionary. She called for more nationalization of British industry, soak-the-rich taxation, and a score of other Socialist proposals . . . The Queen's speech made clear that the [Prime Minister] Wilson government plans to push the wide range of programs drafted or supported by the left wing of the Labor Party and its powerful affiliates in the trade union movement.

With evidence piling up of a gloomy future for private ownership, what is required by utility public relations? First, a clear and intellectually perceptive understanding both of the status of liberal capitalism and democratic representative government in the world, and of whatever steps are being taken to preserve the basic human liberties attached to those concepts. Second, a determination by public relations executives and their superiors to analyze the dimensions of the problem. Third, a commitment to develop company programs dovetailed to a national effort to revitalize the faith of the American people in their political and business institutions.

Admittedly, the latter task will be neither swift nor easy to accomplish, but a creative beginning must be undertaken—and soon. There is no other way, no alternative whatever.

Thematically, it is belaboring the obvious for business leaders to complain continuously of the people's hostility to business, of the educational shortcomings of the colleges, of the crushing burden imposed by governmental regulations. All of these constitute results—not underlying causes. The task is to change men's minds.

Obviously, to do this requires both skill and courage, the imagination to use every available avenue of communication to tell the story of the present business and political system which, though perceptibly imperfect, has carried many Americans triumphantly to the heights of prosperity never before known to man and with the retention of broad personal freedoms. There is a story here and it is the responsibility of public relations to tell it.

Yet no comprehensive communication program can succeed without *identifying the policies and the activities of the nation with the public interest.* Here is stated one of the major elements in any definition of public relations. The business and political establishment has failed signally to do this, and yet it must be done.

Public utilities could well lead the way to a major and public reassessment of our national goals and how to attain them. Their

108   *Crisis of Confidence*

record for past probity suggests their seizing this role. During this cynical period of government and business corruption, when millions of Americans have experienced a sense of betrayal, is it not significant that no public utility has appeared in an unfavorable light?*

It is true, of course, that many utilities have probably diluted the high regard their customers once entertained for them, mainly because of repeated rate increases. It is also true that over the years of the good service they have consistently provided, they have not been publicly involved in the more sordid political scandals. Utilities piled up enough public distrust during the collapse of the Insull empire to last a long time, and only their utter rectitude over decades has re-established their integrity in the eyes of the public.

Thus, while customers may be piqued by their monthly bills, they retain confidence in those who render these statements. They hate the bills but not the companies, if opinion surveys are to be believed.

Seminars of an unusual kind might be held by public relations executives to examine the existing crisis in business and government, avoiding the narcissistic approach which suggests an "all's well with the world" viewpoint. Needed instead is a new and hard-nosed knowledgable confrontation with reality. Too often the tendency has been to kill the messenger of bad tidings while ignoring the message and exalting the purveyor of political cant or demagogic hyperbole. Nor should time be wasted on unproductive complaining about things as they are, for they are that way. The returns are in. The signs are clear, if not to some sheltered executives in corner suites, at least to millions of the unemployed and aged who voice their views in opinion polls and express their frustrations at the ballot box.

Thinking is needed to meet the issues of the times and national leadership is required, creative leadership which can be provided by the public utilities of the nation which have the most to gain because they have the most to lose.

Not everything can be solved, of course. By their very natures

---

*The widely publicized political troubles of the International Telephone & Telegraph Corp. do not properly fall within this context, since the firm, though having utility properties, is really a conglomerate.

some problems will remain insoluble, but they can be isolated and analyzed, and intelligent action planned and taken.

An astonishing dynamism lies dormant in America. Time and again this fact has been recorded in history. Unleashing of this tremendous force for positive change and growth is overdue.

22

The Testing Time

WHEN ANYTHING in nature or industry fails to function it becomes a candidate for obsolescence.

That is why, so they say, that when an ape grew tired of climbing and walked upright his tail atrophied, leaving only vestigial remains at the end of man's spine as a reminder that once he was an arboreal animal. When the horseless carriage arrived, the village blacksmith, an authentic folk hero, became as rare as the whooping crane.

Considering how ruthlessly nature and economics reject discards, one wonders about the future of public relations as a prestigious management function in the utilities industry. Can it survive if found ineffectual in the face of its momentous challenge, one which may prove of epic proportions?

Public relations claims and has repeatedly demonstrated that the role it plays in management, and particularly management decisions, is often of a crucial nature. Now signs are visible that the high tide of effective communications with the public, so admirably helpful at times with issues such as rates, earnings, and threats of public ownership, may have reached its apogee.

Until the present there has been a failure to convince the American consuming public of the unendurable consequences which must flow from a "too little, too late" energy policy.

The specter of scarcity—this new and growing portent of economic disaster—has elicited notably different reactions from three responsible sources: from utility executives, angry frustration in being blocked from a solution; from jurisdictional government agencies, noisy confusion and unwillingness to expedite tedious procedures by cutting red tape, traits not alien to bureaucracies; and from the public, anger and a stubborn refusal to alter a comfortable life style, stemming from the conviction that everything is going to turn out all right anyway, plus a dark suspicion that they may find they have been duped.

At this stage, no one can be *that* sure. Reflecting on the several layers of regulation involved, on the truly stupendous amounts of capital needed for new facilties, on consumers balky over present and contemplated prices, the curious analyst might reasonably raise a chilling question:

Will the nation's energy requirements *ever* be adequately met? And the corollary: *If not, what then?* The answer might well be a catalog of economic horrors too frightening to contemplate.

How frustrating public ignorance and government foot-dragging can be at this critical juncture is described with emphatic clarity by Joseph R. Rensch, president of the Pacific Lighting Corporation, perhaps the world's largest distributor of natural gas in bearing responsibility for serving more than 3,000,000 customers.

Speaking before representatives of a group of California cities in August, 1975, he said that the small user of energy will be the main victim of inordinate delay, warning that the lead time, the period needed to provide additional energy supplies for the market, has already "slipped away."

Bluntly, he added that this slippage occurred while "political and public opinion leaders floundered, dallied and listened to 'instant energy experts' who have come crawling out of the woods by the thousands, each with his own personally guaranteed solution based on windmills, geysers, the ocean tides, animal manure, and signs of the Zodiac. It is easy to proclaim that geothermal, tidal, solar, or barnyard energy is just around the corner. But the lull of complacency created by overly simplistic solutions makes it extremely difficult to convince the public of the need to move rapidly on the hard, realistic energy projects which require long lead times."

In this complaint the perspicacious will discern the signifi-

Crisis of Confidence

cant words "makes it extremely difficult to convince the public." Of what, again? Of the present desperate lack, with time passing every day, maximizing the danger to the ultimate viability of our high energy civilization.

Mr. Rensch has unerringly touched the public relations chord. His comments inferentially suggest that if the public were "convinced" of the need for haste the present barriers to accomplishment could be surmounted and the present "floundering and dallying by political and public opinion leaders" would end.

Clearly, there has been a failure to communicate, persuasively spawning the public skepticism of need. At whose door should this tar baby be dropped?

Confirming Mr. Rensch's view, Burt Wilson, spokesman for CAUSE, an acronym for members of the Campaign Against Utility Services Exploitation, stated in January, 1976, that CAUSE does not believe an energy shortage actually exists. (If this were valid, it would imply the existence of the greatest hoax ever perpetrated on the American consuming public.) In underscoring his view, Mr. Wilson and his cohorts claimed responsibility for helping to abort a plan whereby the Pacific Lighting Corporation hoped to purchase a portion of the Atlantic Richfield Corporation's North Slope gas holdings. Involved in this was a proposal for the gas company to pay the interest on an Arco development loan through small surcharges on customers' bills.

So, as precious time slips away, the nation wrestles with its horrendous problem of finding and delivering energy, a story whose telling places a terrible responsibility upon the public relations executives of the country's utilities. Their greatest task, and severest test, lies ahead—and time is running out.

Epilogue

The Dimensions of Disbelief

I T IS A CLICHE to observe that in the public domain nobody any longer believes anybody about anything.

In one opinion survey after another, Americans express their disenchantment as the nation concludes its Bicentennial and points toward its third century.

No rosy rhetoric by aspiring politicians, soothing promises by the captains of industry, or thundering diatribes by labor's leaders serve to temper the cynical distrust of the man in the street for Big Government, Big Business, or Big Labor. In brief, recent opinion studies as well as angry "Letters of the People" columns in the press suggest that he is not only fed up with all three; in many cases he regards them as enemies.

In this book, attention has been directed almost totally to the communications requirements of utilities, to the problems they must somehow surmount if they are to continue as viable segments of the economic order. Although these utilities are invested with certain special social and legal characteristics, they are components of the general business community. Considerations that affect them apply to the broader picture, particularly in the communications of their problems and activities to their constituent publics. The objective is the creation of understanding, and understanding can be accomplished only through the establishment of credibility.

Credibility is, today, the major problem of business communications programs, as well as those of government and labor. There is a crisis of belief among people . . . a rejection of old values . . . perhaps even an abandonment of faith.

This spiritual malaise is outwardly marked by apathy at the polls. "Why vote? They're all a bunch of crooks, anyway." Taxes become confiscatory, while politicians increase their salaries and fatten their pensions.

Skyward-surging medical and hospital costs,* no problem for the very rich or the very poor, terrorize the middle class, particularly the aged, many of whom no longer knit by the fireplace but languish pitifully in rest homes, some of which are so profit-conscious and noisome as to prompt continuous investigation.

Many converging strands are woven into this tapestry of despair.

Watergate, and the fall of a President, were political and social tragedies. Perhaps they might have been contained were it not for so many other public anxieties. Inflation, with its destruction of savings, the marketing of ever more shoddy merchandise subject to early obsolescence, national and international business bribery scandals . . . these and many more commonplaces of the seventies feed the suspicion that business is corrupt and government is corrupt while labor, with its pension fund thefts, is not far behind.

Bulging welfare rolls cause many to wonder whether, without war, there will ever again be a time of full employment . . . while, with monopolistic industries and monopolistic unions, questions are raised whether the term "free market" is not really an anachronism.

The terrifying net is a monumental decline of trust in government, in business, and in labor—the regnant three of our social, political, and economic system. In our permissive society of the seventies, the church runs a poor fourth. It is not distrusted as much as overlooked, and perhaps that point is significant. Indeed, it may be crucial.

One is loath, even unwilling, to accept the prediction of Michael Harrington and others that we are a decadent society in full

*In its "special health issue" of January 3, 1977, *New West* magazine reported: "Because of cost alone, the present medical system's days are numbered. Already the health care industry is draining off nearly 10 per cent of our gross national product, and prices figure to double in the next five years." *Page 15.*

decline. Yet no sensitive observer of the current scene can deny that *something is happening*, something in the realm of current thought that is dangerous and sinister.

Could a major share of the problem lie in the failure of communication—*truthful* communication—as contrasted to the occasional half-truths of business, government, and labor? No professional publicist worth his salt is unaware that slickness of expression and euphemisms more often than not mark the comments of political men and leaders of business and labor. Dissimulation on a national scale sometimes achieves the status of an art form. Has public relations a responsibility here?

Speaking before the Los Angeles Chapter of the Public Relations Society of America May 21, 1976, Jay Rockey, the Society's National President, announced that "business has a credibility problem" and that "public relations can do one of two things in helping solve it; sit back and wring its hands or assume a position of leadership."

Naturally, he thinks in terms of business, one element of the triad. But all are in the same boat.

They are equally suspect, and while Mr. Rockey, like most of us, is crystal clear on delineating the problem, again, like most of us, he seems a little unclear on providing solutions. In this dilemma what can be done to reestablish credibility for business, government, and labor in the public mind?

The remedy is simplicity itself; but its full application borders on fantasy.

Admitting the modern complexities of business, government, and labor, where secrecy and self interest are usually embraced and full disclosure is often an orphan, the time has long since passed for change.

There must be the development of a new morality for those who deal with the public. . .from the highest government official to the most prestigious business executive and the most lordly labor baron. There must be a reversal of view from the "I'm going to get mine" to "What can I do in the public interest?"

There must be a reversal of drift away from the cynical sophistication of many of those in high places to a realization that there is a sickness in the Republic which can only be cured by a complete change of viewpoint; one which acknowledges that in today's society the public interest and the survival of the systems we believe in are identical.

How can such a drastic reversal be achieved and communicated? There is no easy answer to any new public morality. . .and quite possibly a practical one does not exist. Yet a try must be made, and soon.

It would be ideal if it were to start with national political leadership, with integrity and truth accepted as goals worth striving for within the Presidency, supported both by language and example. A start might be made by opening the secretive, Machiavellian world of national alliances and agreements to public understanding and scrutiny.

It would be ideal if industry and labor were to follow these precepts, perhaps by calling a national conference directed toward making relationships with the public open and honest in every sense. Let us hope that contrived action and linguistic deception would be publicly excoriated in words as hard as cannonballs.

It would be ideal also if public relations men and women, the skilled communicators of our time, were to assume a greater responsibility for public trust than they now possess or practice.

This would be the ideal. Yet we must recognize that it is unlikely to come to full flower overnight. The accepted mores of our well established systems and the quite understandable hunger for personal survival and power of those who labor within them preclude it. The ability to justify and rationalize thought and action dedicated to the self interest and self perpetuation of the corporate body, government and labor alike, has become the regrettable commonplace of our time.

What, then, is the answer? Quite simply, the realization of the nature of the facts that confront us by those in a position to exert influence, and an unshakeable belief that the simple values of integrity and truth must be upheld regardless of personal consequence. It requires neither the fanatic zeal of the evangelist nor the absolutism of the dictatorial view . . . merely the conviction that these values are still real and viable . . . truly imperative to the survival of what we believe in, and are worth every ounce of personal risk to defend and promote.

If we do what we can, it could well be enough.

We must understand that no one can turn back the clock. Never again will we be a raw, new nation drifting Westward to follow a dream of unprecedented growth, blithely accepting the by-products of personal greed as a part of the bargain. Never again can we be a nation of artisans and farmers, concepts still deeply buried in the minds of many, and frequently embellished by pronouncements in the literature of our time. For the artisan has been overwhelmed by General Motors, by IBM and the Bell Laboratories, and the farmer now is a shareholder in a factory in the fields.

So the complexities of our society as it exists today cannot ever again be simplified; and that is one of the first facts we must face unblinkingly as we confront our third century. The second, and more compelling, is that our personal philosophy will determine the outcome.

Browning said, "Truth is within ourselves." And it is.

The knowledge that truth is within each of us, with an understanding that it must be told no matter what the consequences, may counterbalance those dark forces of disbelief that threaten to overwhelm us.

Books Mentioned In The Text

Prologue:
1. Irwin Shaw, *The Image Merchants,* Garden City, N.Y., Doubleday & Company, 1959.

Chapter 1
2. Galbraith, John K., *The Liberal Hour.* New York, New American Library, Mentor Edition, p. 118.

Chapter 2
3. Weiner, Richard, *Professional's Guide to Public Relations Services.* Englewood Cliffs, N.J., Prentice-Hall, Inc., 1975, Third Edition.

Chapter 12
4. Bristol, Lee H., Jr., *Developing the Corporate Image.* New York, Charles Scribner's Sons.
5. Harlow, Rex F., *Social Science in Public Relations.* New York, Harper & Row, 1957.
6. Berelson, Bernard, and Steiner, Gary A., *Human Behavior.* New York, Harcourt Brace Jovanovich, 1963.
7. Hollander, Edwin P., and Hunt, Raymond G., editors, *Current Perspectives in Social Psychology.* New York, Oxford University Press, 1963.

Chapter 15
8. *Environmental Protection Directory.* Chicago, Marquis-Who's Who Books, 1975, Second Edition.
9. *Consumer Protection Directory.* Chicago, Marquis-Who's Who Books, 1975, Second Edition.

Chapter 20
10. Durant, Will and Ariel, *Lessons of History.* New York, Simon & Schuster, 1968, pp. 66, 67.
11. Galbraith, John K., *The New Industrial State.* New York, New American Library, Signet Edition, 1968, p. 399.
12. Harrington, Michael, *The Accidental Century.* New York, Penguin Books, Pelican Edition, 1967, p. 13.

BIBLIOGRAPHY

Abelson, Herbert L., *Persuasion*. New York, Springer Publishing Co., 1959.

Baus, Herbert M., *Publicity in Action*. New York, Harper & Brothers, 1942.

Bernays, Edward L., *Public Relations*. Norman, Okla., University of Oklahoma Press, 1952.

Cameron, John, and Aspley, L.F., Editors, *The Dartnell Public Relations Handbook*. Chicago, The Dartnell Corporation, 1956.

Harlow, Rex F., and Black, Marvin M., *Practical Public Relations*. New York, Harper & Brothers, 1947 (Revised).

Hollander, E.P., and Hunt, Raymond G., *Current Perspectives in Social Psychology*. New York, Oxford University Press, 1963.

Lane, Robert E., and Sears, David O., *Public Opinion*. Englewood Cliffs, N.J., Prentice-Hall, Inc., 1964.

Packard, Vance, *The Hidden Persuaders*. New York, David McKay Co., Inc., 1957.

Strunk, William, Jr., *The Elements of Style*. New York, The Macmillan Company, 1959.

Index

Index

Index

"....the time has long